Jon Speelman's
Chess Puzzle Book

Jon Speelman

Julian Hodgson
for Henry.

GAMBIT

First published in the UK by Gambit Publications Ltd 2008

ISBN-13: 978-1-904600-96-1
ISBN-10: 1-904600-96-4

DISTRIBUTION:
Worldwide (except USA): Central Books Ltd, 99 Wallis Rd, London E9 5LN, England. Tel +44 (0)20 8986 4854 Fax +44 (0)20 8533 5821.
E-mail: orders@Centralbooks.com

Gambit Publications Ltd, 99 Wallis Rd, London E9 5LN, England.
E-mail: info@gambitbooks.com
Website (regularly updated): www.gambitbooks.com

Edited by Graham Burgess
Typeset by John Nunn
Cover image by Wolff Morrow
Printed in Great Britain by The Cromwell Press, Trowbridge, Wilts.

10 9 8 7 6 5 4 3 2 1

Gambit Publications Ltd
Managing Director: Murray Chandler GM
Chess Director: Dr John Nunn GM
Editorial Director: Graham Burgess FM
German Editor: Petra Nunn WFM
Webmaster: Dr Helen Milligan WFM

Contents

Symbols

+	check
++	double check
#	checkmate
!!	brilliant move
!	good move
!?	interesting move
?!	dubious move
?	bad move
??	blunder
Ch	championship
corr.	correspondence game
1-0	the game ends in a win for White
½-½	the game ends in a draw
0-1	the game ends in a win for Black
(D)	see next diagram

Introduction

When John Nunn persuaded me to write a book on tactics I was initially rather dubious since there are already many of them on the market. But as I prepared finally to put finger to keyboard I became rather more optimistic since I do think that there is a fairly simple message which is worth hammering home: tactics is a combination of vision and calculation; both are necessary and neither is obvious – even to the best players – during the hurly burly of practical play.

The vision results from pattern recognition which you then process to generate possible moves. It's a subconscious process which no doubt has a deep underlying scientific theory, but the practical effect for chess-players is that by practising – going through examples from a book such as this – you get better at seeing the moves which may – and I stress *may* – work.

Calculation is the part where you verify whether they really do. It's important to understand that whereas in a book the examples are generally chosen to be successful, in real life you don't know *a priori* whether some beautiful combinative idea is the path to success or merely a figment of your imagination – all you can do is try to verify your idea.

While in the utopian – or possibly dystopian – world of Alexander Kotov, this involved calculating each branch of the 'tree of analysis' exactly once, in the real world, or certainly the one I inhabit, there are often times when you look at a line and fail to find something but have a hunch that it ought to work and go back to it. What is harmful though is going back again and again, desperately willing there to be something and so using up too much clock time in vain.

Since I believe that the message is fairly simple, I've deliberately chosen reasonably simple or at least clear examples for the main part. I grew up solving hundreds of small tactical puzzles from books and magazines and have always felt that the best way to progress is not by hurling yourself at some massive brick wall but rather by picking daintily through a series of slight but satisfying obstacles, overcoming each of which gives you a small but pleasant buzz of success.

I've divided the material into two main sections: The Elements and Tactics in Practice. In the first the positions are sorted by their underlying tactical theme – so that you know what you're looking for; while the second consists of three large 'tests' going up from 'Finger Exercises' via a 'Mixed Bag' to a final section of 'Tougher Examples'.

Improving your tactical skill is a far from magical process and I hope that readers will enjoy doing so by using this book.

Part 1: The Elements

Knight Forks

I've started with the knight fork since it is one of the most ubiquitous tactical elements. As the only 'leaper' in normal chess (there are lots of others in the problem world), the knight is able to attack any other piece without itself being under threat.

It's a confusing piece for beginners, and indeed very experienced players too can find the knight difficult to play against, especially, for example, in endgames in which the opponent has two of the beasts; or in a middlegame in which it suddenly goes somewhere unexpected, not necessarily initiating an immediate fork but preparing to attack.

In any case, I'll start as in all chapters in this section with simple examples and build up to more challenging ones.

KF01 White to play
(Solution: see page 94)

KF02 White to play
Here White has to do more work since the fork has to be set up.
(Solution: see page 94)

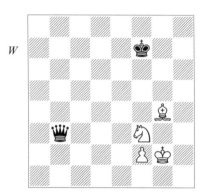

KF03 White to play

This is very similar to the previous exercise but with the bishop effecting the deflection.

(Solution: see page 94)

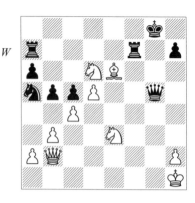

KF05 White to play

(Solution: see page 94)

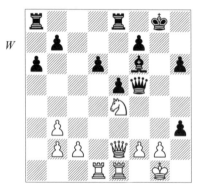

KF04 White to play

We move on to a practical example in which the principle is the same though the presence of so many pieces obscures it.

(Solution: see page 94)

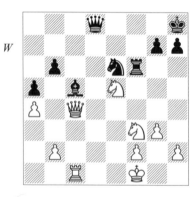

KF06 White to play

A pawn down, Black is rocking here but there looks still to be plenty of fight in the position. How did White prove otherwise?

(Solution: see page 95)

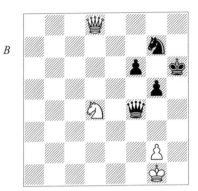

KF07 Black to play

Black blundered with 51...g4??. What was the response?

(Solution: see page 95)

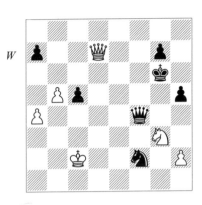

KF09 White to play

With queens and knights flying about, this position looks very unclear but White found a way to force simplification to a won ending. How?

(Solution: see page 95)

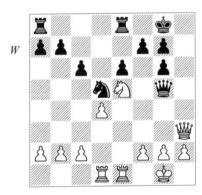

KF08 White to play

The black position looks pretty solid but White was able immediately to win a vital pawn. How?

(Solution: see page 95)

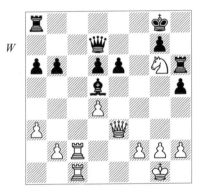

KF10 White to play

White obviously has a huge advantage, but what is the cleanest way to win (obviously using a knight fork) and how does White clean up if Black avoids the fork?

(Solution: see page 95)

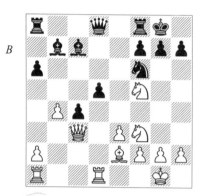

KF11 Black to play

One of the greatest players in history committed a rare blunder here with 20...♗c8??. What was the response winning two pawns?

(Solution: see page 95)

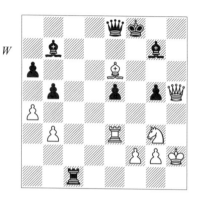

KF13 White to play

In this rather messier position White is all over Black on the light squares but still has to connect. What is the cleanest win with a sequence in which a knight fork is integral?

(Solution: see page 95)

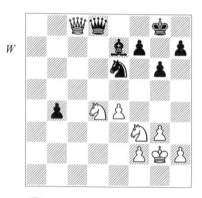

KF12 White to play

Black's last move was 50...♕d6-d8?? What is the reply?

(Solution: see page 95)

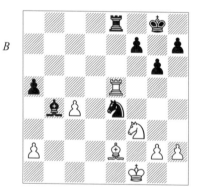

KF14 Black to play

In a blitz game, Black played the natural-looking 26...♖xe5, overlooking something much better. What?

(Solution: see page 95)

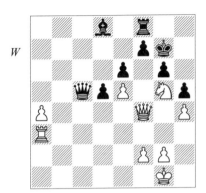

KF15 White to play

This is also from a blitz game, which by their very nature strip chess bare and so tend to highlight simple tactics. How did White set up a knight fork?

(Solution: see page 96)

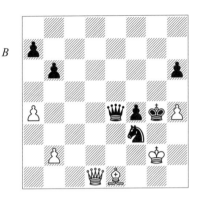

KF17 Black to play
(Solution: see page 96)

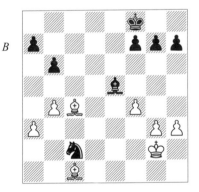

KF16 Black to play

Endgames with bishop and knight vs two bishops can be extremely unpleasant to defend, especially against a good technician as White was here. However, Black found an immediate bail-out. What was it?

(Solution: see page 96)

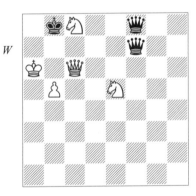

KF18 White to play

This is the end of a study. What is the main line?

(Solution: see page 96)

Loose Pieces

In this section we look at a variety of methods of exploiting the opponent's loose pieces.

While it's sometimes a necessity to leave pieces without protection, experienced players try to minimize this. One loose piece gives the opponent a potential tempo to attack it and improve his position in some other way; while if there are two (or more) then there is serious potential trouble since both may be attacked simultaneously.

In the previous chapter we examined knight forks. Here we look first at forks by other pieces, most often, due to its great mobility, the queen. Discovered attacks whereby a piece opens a 'battery' – unmasking an attack from a rook, bishop or queen behind it – are another way of making two threats simultaneously. This 'battery' attack may be a check – making it a discovered check; and occasionally it's possible for both the battery and the piece moving to give check, adding up to a 'double check' – the atom bomb of chess tactics – though this normally occurs during mating attacks rather than combinations for mere material gain.

We start with the outcome of an uncharacteristic blunder by a great player:

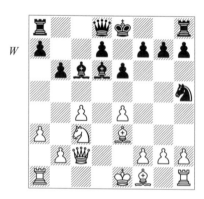

LP01 White to play
(Solution: see page 97)

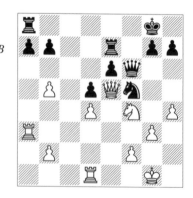

LP02 Black to play
Black played 27...b6. Why was this not a good idea?
(Solution: see page 97)

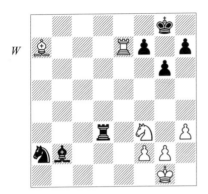

LP03 White to play
(Solution: see page 97)

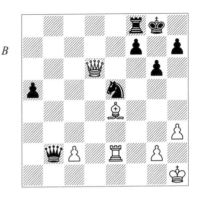

LP05 Black to play
(Solution: see page 97)

LP04 White to play
White now played 24 ♗xg7 ♚xg7.
How did he follow up?
(Solution: see page 97)

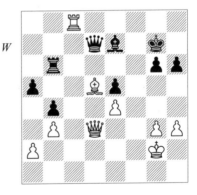

LP06 White to play
The black queen and rook are both
loose. White can gain a big advantage
by exploiting the former and has a
complete knockout blow using the latter. What are the two lines (which both
start the same)?
(Solution: see page 97)

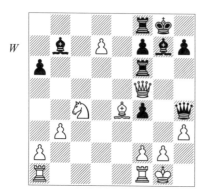

LP07 White to play
(Solution: see page 98)

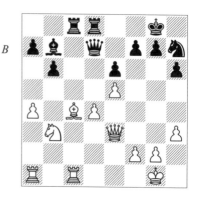

LP09 Black to play
White had just played 23 ♘d2-b3?.
Not a good idea, but why not?
(Solution: see page 98)

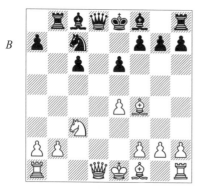

LP08 Black to play
In this position (which is obviously
still in the opening) Black blundered
with 11...♖xb2??. Why was this wrong?
(Solution: see page 98)

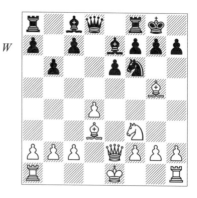

LP10 White to play
(Solution: see page 98)

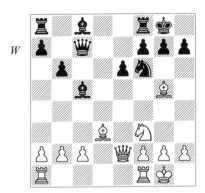

LP11 White to play
Can White win material?
(Solution: see page 98)

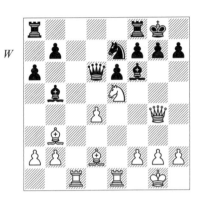

LP13 White to play
White opened fire with the highly thematic 20 ♘xf7 ♖xf7 21 ♖xe6 and Black tried 21...♛d7. What was the response?
(Solution: see page 99)

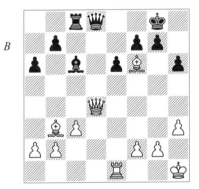

LP12 Black to play
In an unpleasant position, Black recaptured with the queen (23...♛xf6). How did White proceed?
(Solution: see page 99)

LP14 White to play
White incautiously lopped off a pawn with 15 ♛d5+ ♚h8 16 ♛xc5 (if 16 ♛xe5, then 16...♖fe8). How was this drastically refuted?
(Solution: see page 99)

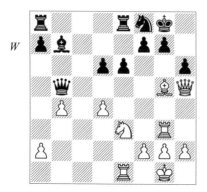

LP15 White to play

How can White get out of the pin and use a vicious mechanism to win material?

(Solution: see page 99)

Opening and Closing Lines

In order for chess pieces (apart from the knight) to operate effectively, they require open lines. A lot of tactical play therefore concerns itself with manoeuvres to open lines for your own pieces and/or close ones which the enemy wishes to use. These can generally be subsumed under other topics but here I'm gathering a few together to highlight this particular aspect.

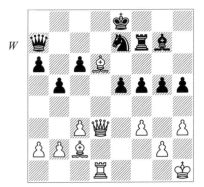

LO01 White to play
(Solution: see page 99)

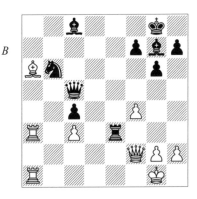

LO02 Black to play
(Solution: see page 100)

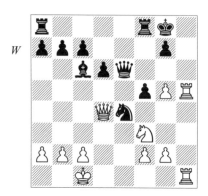

LO03 White to play
(Solution: see page 100)

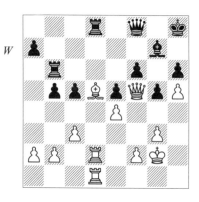

LO05 White to play
(Solution: see page 100)

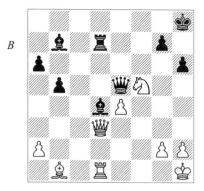

LO04 Black to play
In this famous position Black re-signed. Why was this premature?
(Solution: see page 100)

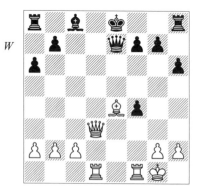

LO06 White to play
(Solution: see page 100)

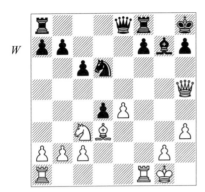

LO07 White to play
(Solution: see page 100)

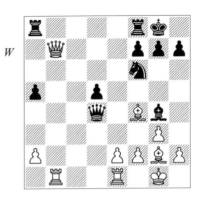

LO09 White to play
(Solution: see page 101)

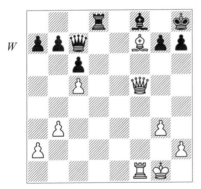

LO08 White to play
(Solution: see page 101)

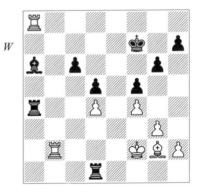

LO10 White to play
(Solution: see page 101)

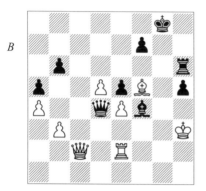

LO11 Black to play
(Solution: see page 101)

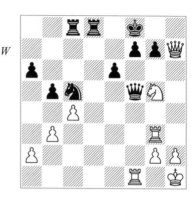

LO13 White to play
(Solution: see page 102)

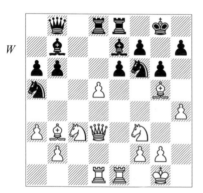

LO12 White to play

What is the move White wants to make and (without going into too much detail) does it work?

(Solution: see page 101)

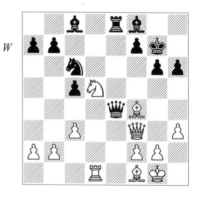

LO14 White to play
(Solution: see page 102)

LO15 White to play
(Solution: see page 102)

Pins

The pin is one of the most powerful elements in a chess-player's tactical armoury since a pinned piece, by virtue of its inability to move, can easily become a serious target. However, it is very important to appreciate the difference between an absolute pin against the king, in which the pinned piece is prevented from moving by the Laws of Chess, and a relative pin, in which the piece can't move without exposing an important unit behind it, such as the queen, but may nevertheless be able to jump away as part of a tactical counter-operation.

We start with something extremely simple.

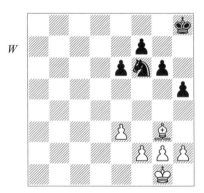

PI01 White to play

a) Is there any difference if the h5-pawn is on h6?

(Solution: see page 102)

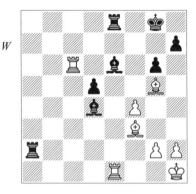

PI02 White to play

(Solution: see page 102)

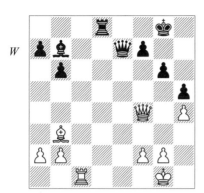

PI03 White to play
(Solution: see page 102)

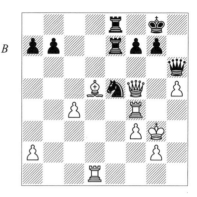

PI05 Black to play

White had already twice put his queen on g6 utilizing the pin. Black now played 36...g6?. Why was this a decisive error?

(Solution: see page 103)

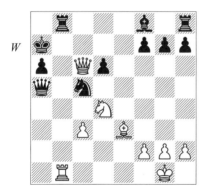

PI04 White to play
(Solution: see page 102)

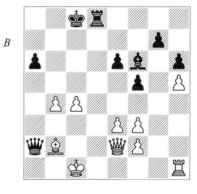

PI06 Black to play
(Solution: see page 103)

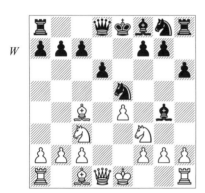

PI07 White to play
(Solution: see page 103)

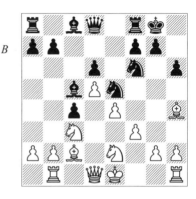

PI09 Black to play
(Solution: see page 103)

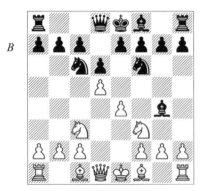

PI08 Black to play
Is 5...♘e5 at all possible and why?
(Solution: see page 103)

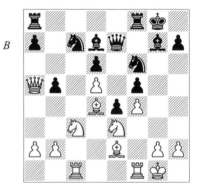

PI10 Black to play
Black played 20...♖fc8 and later drew. Why is 20...♘cxd5 bad?
(Solution: see page 104)

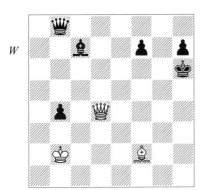

PI11 White to play
(Solution: see page 104)

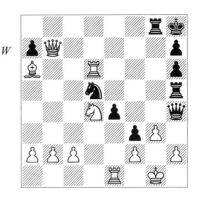

PI13 White to play
White seems about to be mated but
has a combinative way to escape. What
is it?

(Solution: see page 104)

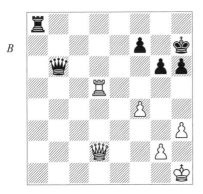

PI12 Black to play
Black starts with 1...♖a1+ 2 ♔h2
♕g1+ 3 ♔g3 ♖a3+. Then 4 ♔g4 ♕h2
5 ♕f2 ♖xh3 should win for Black, but
what is the answer to 4 ♖d3?

(Solution: see page 104)

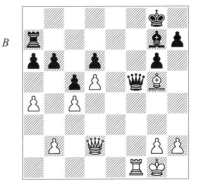

PI14 Black to play
After 23...♗d4+ 24 ♗e3 Black continued 24...♕g5. Why wasn't this as
clever as it looked?

(Solution: see page 104)

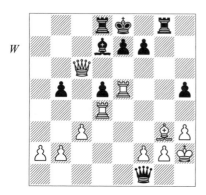

PI15 White to play

White created a pin with 1 ♖exd5 so that if 1...♗xc6, then 2 ♖xd8#. How did Black reply?

(Solution: see page 104)

Skewers

The skewer is another extremely potent tactical weapon at the chess-player's disposal. Generally, it will involve the king being checked and when it moves out of the way, some unit behind it perishing, but a skewer can also sometimes be effective if some other high-value piece is attacked and has to flee.

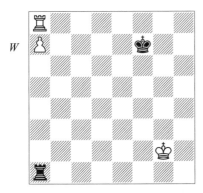

SK01 White to play
(Solution: see page 104)

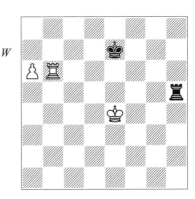

SK02 White to play
(Solution: see page 104)

B

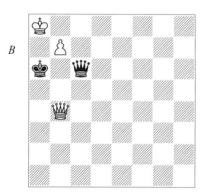

SK03 Black to play
How does White answer 1...♕d5,
1...♕f3 or 1...♕g2?
(Solution: see page 104)

W

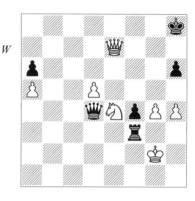

SK05 White to play
(Solution: see page 105)

W

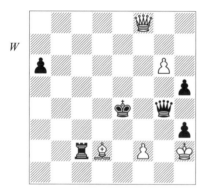

SK04 White to play
(Solution: see page 105)

B

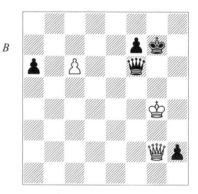

SK06 Black to play
(Solution: see page 105)

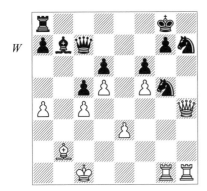

SK07 White to play
(Solution: see page 105)

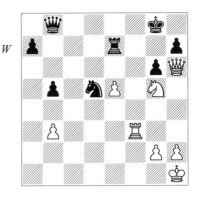

SK09 White to play
(Solution: see page 105)

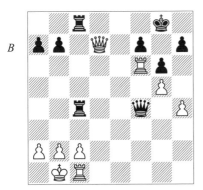

SK08 Black to play
(Solution: see page 105)

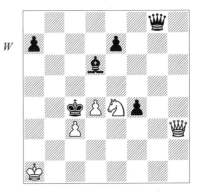

SK10 White to play
(Solution: see page 106)

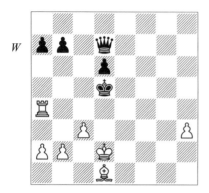

SK11 White to play

The main line is very short but also very pretty.

(Solution: see page 106)

SK12 White to play

(Solution: see page 106)

Overloaded Pieces and Deflections

Ideally when playing chess, both sides try to avoid loose pieces and keep everything important safely defended. In the heat of battle, however, this is very hard to achieve and there will often be moments when one player or other has loose unit(s) from which the opponent can try to profit by attacking.

Pieces may also become committed to defending some crucial weakness – such as a pawn or square near to the king or the back rank – in which case they become prime targets and positively invite a tactical action to disturb them.

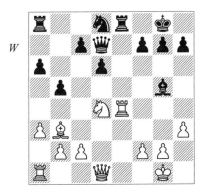

OL01 White to play
(Solution: see page 106)

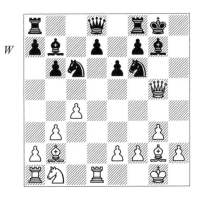

OL02 White to play
(Solution: see page 106)

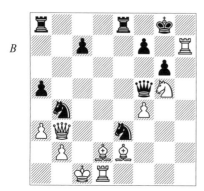

OL03 Black to play
(Solution: see page 106)

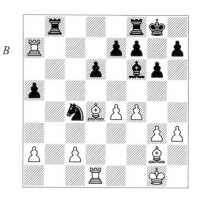

OL05 Black to play
(Solution: see page 107)

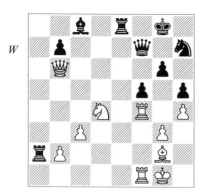

OL04 White to play
(Solution: see page 106)

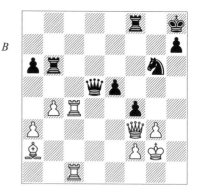

OL06 Black to play
(Solution: see page 107)

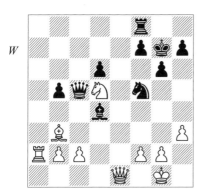

OL07 White to play
White played 26 c3?. Why was this natural-looking move a fatal mistake?
(Solution: see page 107)

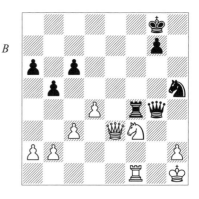

OL09 Black to play
What is the first move Black should consider here, and why does it work?
(Solution: see page 107)

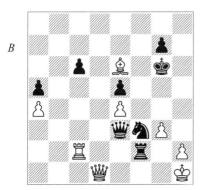

OL08 Black to play
Black is winning pretty easily but found a pretty short-cut using a deflection. What was it?
(Solution: see page 107)

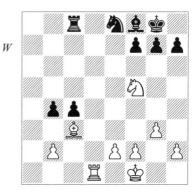

OL10 White to play
How did White force a draw?
(Solution: see page 107)

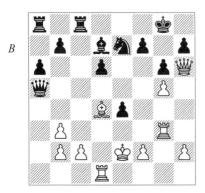

B

OL11 Black to play
(Solution: see page 107)

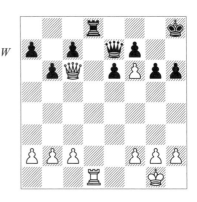

W

OL13 White to play
(Solution: see page 108)

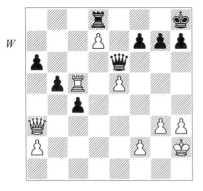

W

OL12 White to play
How did White exploit his passed pawn and Black's weak back rank?
(Solution: see page 108)

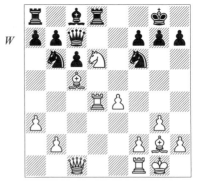

W

OL14 White to play
With the two bishops and a space advantage, White has a clear advantage but it's far from obvious that he can force victory in just two more moves. How?
(Solution: see page 108)

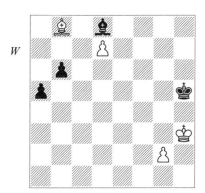

OL15 White to play
(Solution: see page 108)

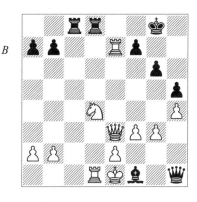

OL17 Black to play
(Solution: see page 108)

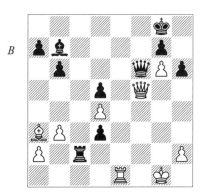

OL16 Black to play
(Solution: see page 108)

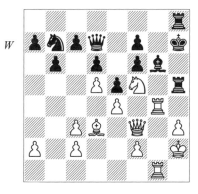

OL18 White to play
(Solution: see page 109)

Mating Attacks

In order for a mating attack to be successful against competent defence, the attacker needs to have some sort of decisive advantage.

One possibility is overwhelming force, but this normally won't be especially interesting – he'll be able to finish the opponent off more or less as he chooses. More likely in a competitive game there will be some target(s) near the king which the attacker can fix on and the defender cannot cover adequately.

In many cases these will amount to a weak colour complex. In the case of a black king castled kingside, this will either be all the dark squares in front of the king – f6, h6 and crucially g7; or the light squares: one or both of h7 and f7.

There are also specific weak spots before castling, most notably f2 and f7, patterns specifically relating to queenside castling (MA30) and extremely specific mating sequences such as smothered mate (MA23 and MA24). And the back rank generates so many beautiful combinations that I've put it in a separate chapter.

I'll start with attacks against the uncastled king and the perennial weak spots on f7 and f2.

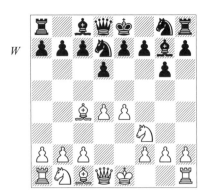

MA01 White to play
(Solution: see page 109)

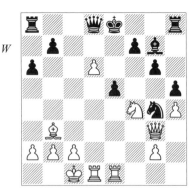

MA02 White to play
(Solution: see page 109)

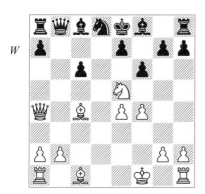

MA03 White to play
(Solution: see page 109)

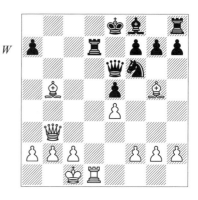

MA04 White to play
(Solution: see page 109)

The uncastled king can also come under attack if the centre opens too early and the opponent gains a lead in development, as the next two examples demonstrate.

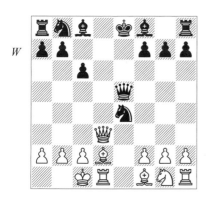

MA05 White to play
(Solution: see page 110)

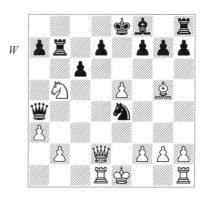

MA06 White to play
(Solution: see page 110)

We move on to the castled king.

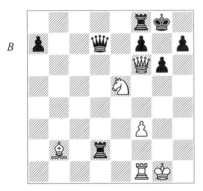

MA07 Black to play

In this obviously made-up example, how does White answer a) 1...♕h3 and b) 1...♕e6?

(Solution: see page 110)

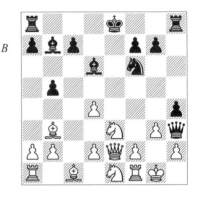

MA09 Black to play
(Solution: see page 110)

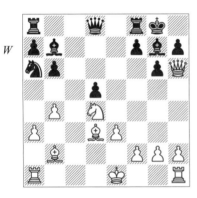

MA08 White to play
(Solution: see page 110)

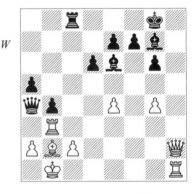

MA10 White to play
What is the cleanest win?
(Solution: see page 110)

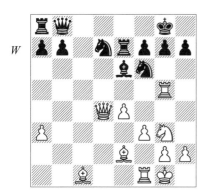

MA11 White to play
(Solution: see page 111)

MA13 White to play
(Solution: see page 111)

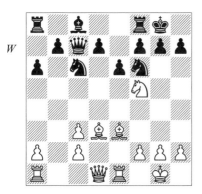

MA12 White to play

In this rather harder example, what move is crying out to be played and what is the follow-up (White's next move is the important one)?

(Solution: see page 111)

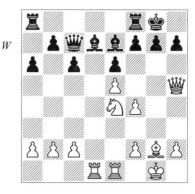

MA14 White to play
(Solution: see page 111)

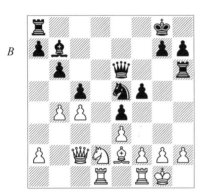

MA15 Black to play
(Solution: see page 112)

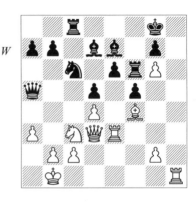

MA17 White to play
(Solution: see page 112)

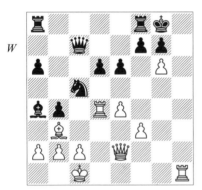

MA16 White to play
(Solution: see page 112)

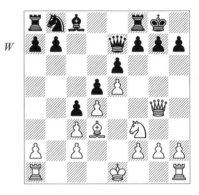

MA18 White to play
(Solution: see page 112)

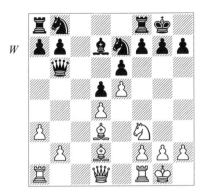

MA19 White to play

In this more typical example Black has more latitude in defence. Obviously White starts 12 ♗xh7+ ♔xh7 13 ♘g5+.

a) After 13...♔g8 why is it helpful (though far from essential) that the pawn is on a3 rather than a2?

b) In the other lines why is it very important that the black knight is on b8?

(Solution: see page 112)

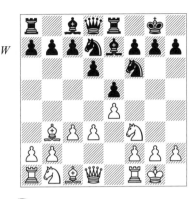

MA21 White to play
(Solution: see page 113)

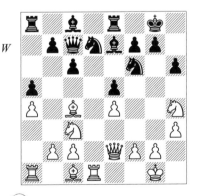

MA20 White to play
(Solution: see page 113)

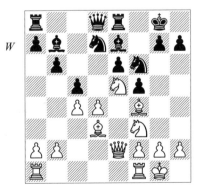

MA22 White to play
(Solution: see page 113)

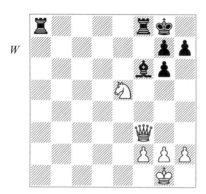

MA23 White to play
(Solution: see page 113)

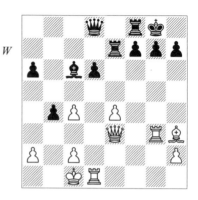

MA25 White to play
(Solution: see page 113)

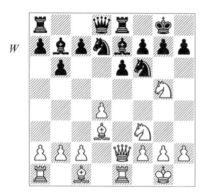

MA24 White to play
(Solution: see page 113)

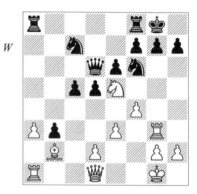

MA26 White to play
(Solution: see page 114)

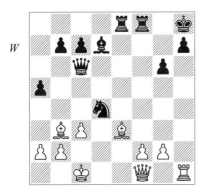

MA27 White to play

The obvious recapture on d4 is very strong but White found something even better. What was it?

(Solution: see page 114)

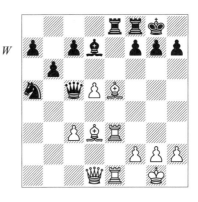

MA29 White to play
(Solution: see page 114)

MA28 White to play
(Solution: see page 114)

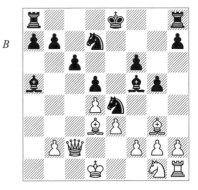

MA30 Black to play

Black now blundered by 19...0-0-0. What was the reply?

(Solution: see page 114)

The Back Rank

The prevalence of back-rank combinations is surely a consequence of the castling rule – otherwise it would take far too much effort regularly to get the king behind an 'ideal' barrier of three pawns.

Given that just a single rook can deliver a knockout blow, material is worth little during back-rank combinations and they often feature apparently paradoxical sequences in which some sort of diabolical deflection is employed to lure the poor rook or queen from its duty, exposing the king to a deadly sideways blow.

We start, however, with something relatively straightforward.

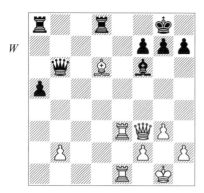

BR01 White to play
(Solution: see page 115)

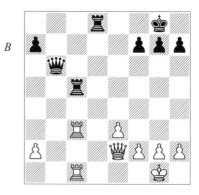

BR02 Black to play
(Solution: see page 115)

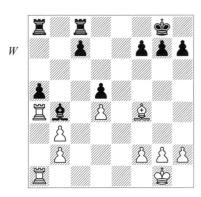

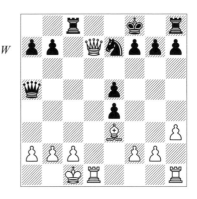

BR03 White to play
White chose 1 ♗xc7. Was this inspired or disastrous?
(Solution: see page 115)

BR05 White to play
What was White's next devastating move? (There are several good follow-ups.)
(Solution: see page 115)

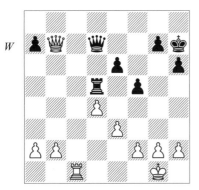

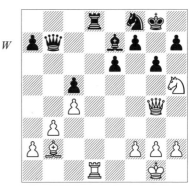

BR04 White to play
White apparently finished the game with one mighty blow: 1 ♖c7. But did Black have to resign?
(Solution: see page 115)

BR06 White to play
White chose the enticing 23 ♘f6+ ♗xf6 24 ♗xf6 but what was the reply?
(Solution: see page 116)

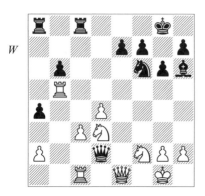

BR07 White to play
In a bad position White tried 25 ♕xe7. How did Black reply?
(Solution: see page 116)

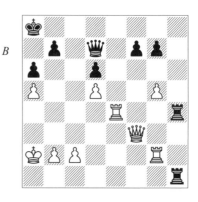

BR09 Black to play
(Solution: see page 116)

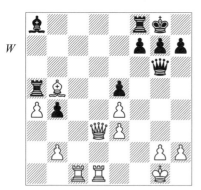

BR08 White to play
(Solution: see page 116)

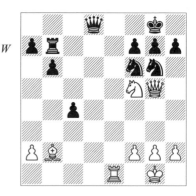

BR10 White to play
(Solution: see page 116)

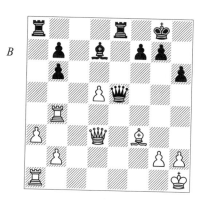

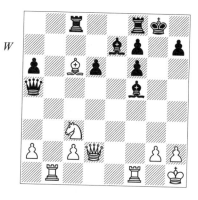

BR11 Black to play
(Solution: see page 116)

BR12 White to play

White attempted to trade blow for blow with 19 ♗b7 ♖xc3 20 ♖xf5, but what came next?

(Solution: see page 117)

Stalemate

Although most of the rules of modern chess, including castling, had been established by the 17th century, attitudes to stalemate took longer to crystallize, with some considering the act of giving stalemate an 'inferior win' and others a 'dishonourable loss'. Indeed in England it wasn't until the London Chess Club Laws of 1807 that it was generally agreed to be a draw.

This status has a profound effect on endgame theory. For example, if stalemate were a win then king and pawn vs king would generally be won (unless the defender could actually capture the pawn) as would 'bishop and wrong rook's pawn' vs king.

Stalemate is essentially a strategic defensive weapon in the endgame but also occurs in numerous endgame studies and as a surprise tactical defensive resource in seemingly hopeless positions with more pieces on the board. A number of these are sprinkled throughout the second part of this book, but for the moment here are a few standard and reasonably clear examples.

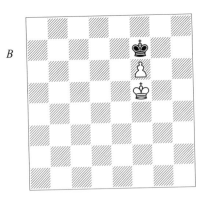

ST01 Black to play
(Solution: see page 117)

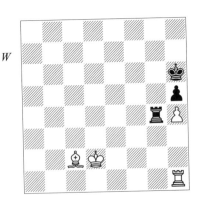

ST02 White to play
Why was 1 ♔e3 a mistake?
(Solution: see page 117)

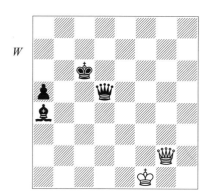

ST03 White to play
(Solution: see page 117)

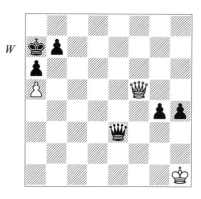

ST05 White to play
(Solution: see page 118)

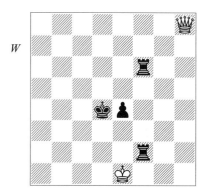

ST04 White to play
(Solution: see page 117)

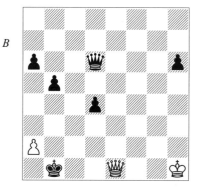

ST06 Black to play
(Solution: see page 118)

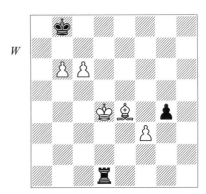

W

ST07 White to play
Should the king go to e5 or e3?
(Solution: see page 118)

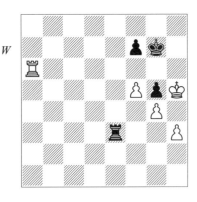

W

ST09 White to play
(Solution: see page 118)

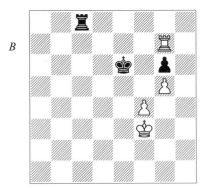

B

ST08 Black to play
(Solution: see page 118)

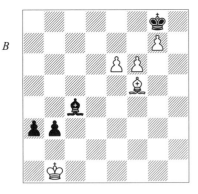

B

ST10 Black to play
(Solution: see page 118)

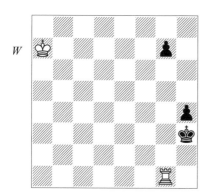

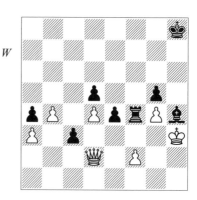

ST11 White to play
(Solution: see page 119)

ST12 White to play
Can White capture on c3?
(Solution: see page 119)

Pawn Promotion

The energy release when a pawn is promoted is so great that in the run-up to this, minor material considerations are generally no object.

Combinative play is therefore extremely common either to force the promotion of one of your own passed pawns or prevent an enemy one's coronation; or to influence a race in your favour, arranging that when you do promote it's in particularly favourable circumstances – for example, with check.

We start with one of the fundamental positions of endgame theory: a classic pawn breakthrough.

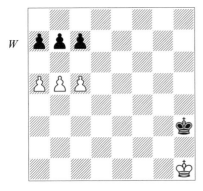

PP01

a) White to play.

b) How can Black defend if it is his move?

(Solution: see page 119)

PP02 White to play
(Solution: see page 119)

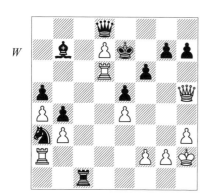

PP03 White to play
What is the cleanest win?
(Solution: see page 119)

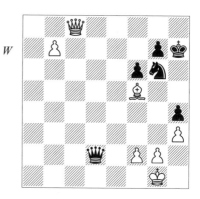

PP05 White to play
(Solution: see page 119)

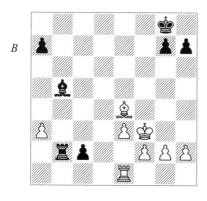

PP04 Black to play
(Solution: see page 119)

PP06 White to play
(Solution: see page 120)

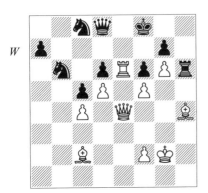

PP07 White to play
(Solution: see page 120)

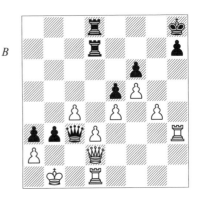

PP09 Black to play
(Solution: see page 120)

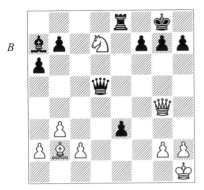

PP08 Black to play
(Solution: see page 120)

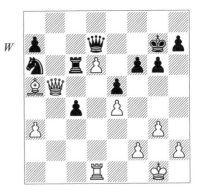

PP10 White to play
(Solution: see page 120)

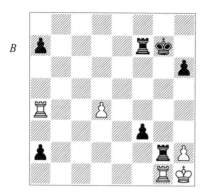

PP11 Black to play
(The second move is the important one.)
(Solution: see page 120)

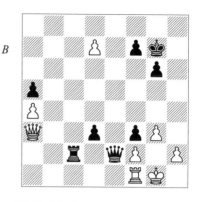

PP13 Black to play
What result?
(Solution: see page 121)

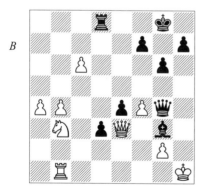

PP12 Black to play
What is the cleanest (and most aesthetically pleasing) win?
(Solution: see page 121)

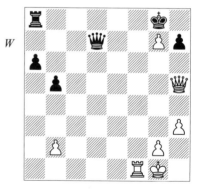

PP14 White to play
(Solution: see page 121)

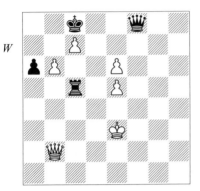

PP15 White to play
(Solution: see page 121)

Part 2: Tactics in Practice

Finger Exercises

This section comprises 48 positions, in which the main task is to see the combinative blow that is available. Often during a game you will have an idea but then wonder whether it works. Here once you do find it then the resultant play is generally extremely clear.

The examples therefore are short and quite 'simple'. However, having the vision is an absolutely essential precursor to tactical mastery.

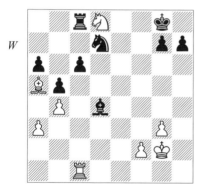

FE01 White to play

There is an obvious skewer but does it lead to anything?

(Solution: see page 121)

FE02 Black to play

(Solution: see page 122)

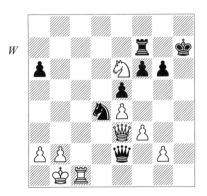

FE03 White to play

Black has just tried 34...♔g7-h7? (34...♔g8 was a better chance). What came next?

(Solution: see page 122)

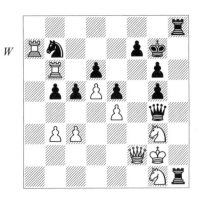

FE05 White to play
(Solution: see page 122)

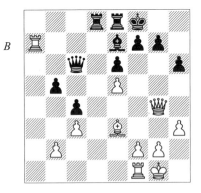

FE04 Black to play

Black attempted to free himself with 24...♗c5. Why was this not a good idea?

(Solution: see page 122)

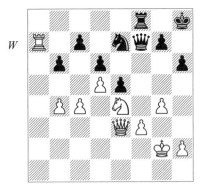

FE06 White to play

What should White not do, and why?

(Solution: see page 122)

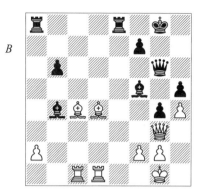

FE07 Black to play

Black now chose the plausible move 27...♗c2. Why was this not a good idea?

(Solution: see page 122)

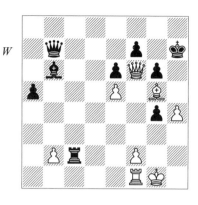

FE09 White to play

Black is about to destroy White's kingside but it is White to move and he can get in his blow first. What was it and why can't Black counterattack?

(Solution: see page 123)

FE08 Black to play

Black's connected passed pawns are huge but at the moment White is threatening ♖c8+. How did Black repel this threat to force victory?

(Solution: see page 122)

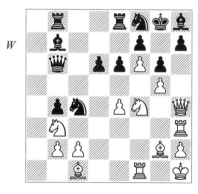

FE10 White to play
(Solution: see page 123)

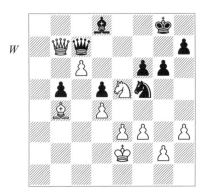

W

FE11 White to play

Obviously Black is under heavy pressure here but how did White finish off immediately?

(Solution: see page 123)

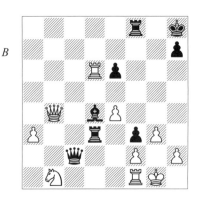

B

FE13 Black to play

(Solution: see page 123)

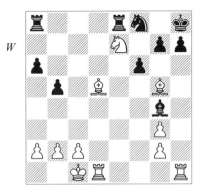

W

FE12 White to play

(Solution: see page 123)

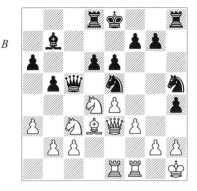

B

FE14 Black to play

(Solution: see page 123)

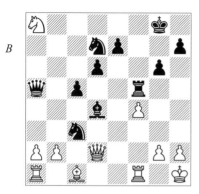

FE15 Black to play
(Solution: see page 124)

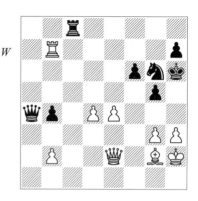

FE17 White to play
White is surely winning, but what is the best and most aesthetically pleasing way to complete the victory?
(Solution: see page 124)

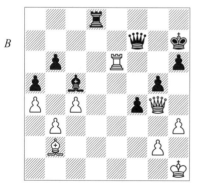

FE16 Black to play
(Solution: see page 124)

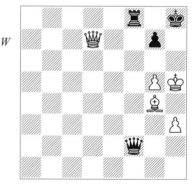

FE18 White to play
Despite the small material disadvantage, White should surely draw. However, he now tried for more with the ambitious 61 ♔g6. Why was this a very bad idea?
(Solution: see page 124)

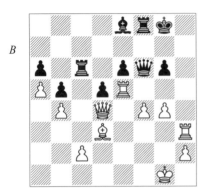

FE19 Black to play

Under massive pressure, Black tried 40...♕xf4. What was the response?

(Solution: see page 124)

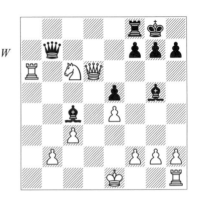

FE21 White to play

a) The obvious move is 23 ♖a7 but this runs into a counter which at least complicates matters. What is it?

b) White instead found a much better way to wrap things up. How?

(Solution: see page 124)

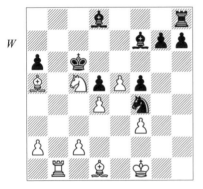

FE20 White to play

White is clearly doing well here, but what is the very best continuation?

(Solution: see page 124)

FE22 Black to play

a) What suggests that there might be a combination in the air?

b) How did Black take advantage?

(Solution: see page 124)

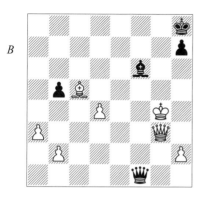

FE23 Black to play

White has just blundered with 57 ♔h3-g4??. Given that this is a quiz book, Black's devastating reply should be obvious.

(Solution: see page 125)

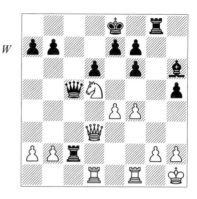

FE25 White to play

Black has won a pawn and his rook is on the seventh rank but his forces are rather scattered. How did White take advantage?

(Solution: see page 125)

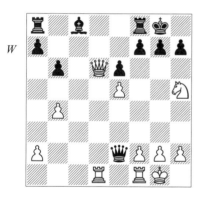

FE24 White to play

What is the obvious try and does it work?

(Solution: see page 125)

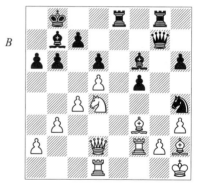

FE26 Black to play

White has just guarded g2 with 26 ♖f1-f2 but this created a weakness on the back rank. How did Black now force a win?

(Solution: see page 125)

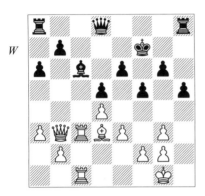

FE27 White to play

White opted for 20 ♕d1 and later lost. What should he have done?

(Solution: see page 125)

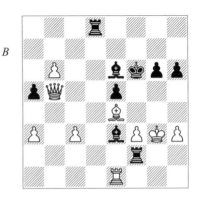

FE29 Black to play

It's fairly obvious what Black would like to play, but can you see the follow-up?

(Solution: see page 126)

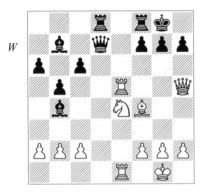

FE28 White to play
(Solution: see page 126)

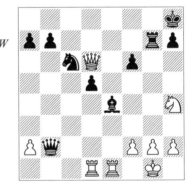

FE30 White to play
(Solution: see page 126)

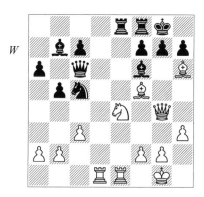

FE31 White to play
(Solution: see page 126)

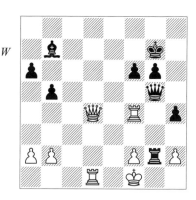

FE33 White to play
(Solution: see page 126)

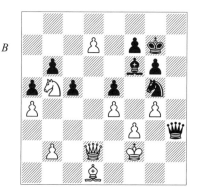

FE32 Black to play

Black chose 35...♘e6, and won in ten more moves, but in doing so he had missed an instant knockout. What?

(Solution: see page 126)

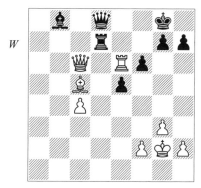

FE34 White to play
(Solution: see page 126)

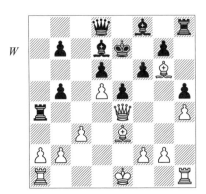

FE35 White to play
(Solution: see page 126)

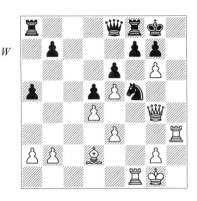

FE37 White to play
(Solution: see page 127)

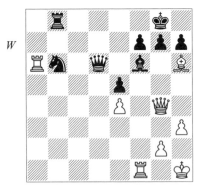

FE36 White to play

White has a material advantage but with all the material on the kingside it looks as though winning will be a very long hard struggle, if possible at all. However, a nice combination finished matters instantly. What was it?

(Solution: see page 126)

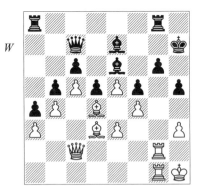

FE38 White to play

All of White's pieces are placed optimally so he must calculate to see if there is a way to break through. What is the obvious way to do so and does it work?

(Solution: see page 127)

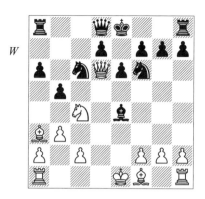

FE39 White to play

Black is a pawn up but has weak dark squares. If the c4-knight moves, he should be able to consolidate but White found a splendid way to cash in immediately. What was it?

(Solution: see page 127)

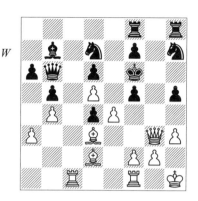

FE41 White to play

Black's position is hanging by a thread. How did White cut it?

(Solution: see page 127)

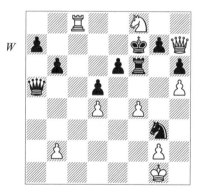

FE40 White to play

With ...♛e1+ in the air, Black seems to have escaped, but White found a beautiful move which proved otherwise. What was it?

(Solution: see page 127)

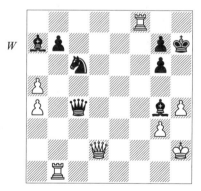

FE42 White to play

(Solution: see page 127)

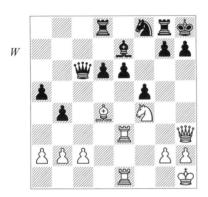

FE43 White to play
(Solution: see page 127)

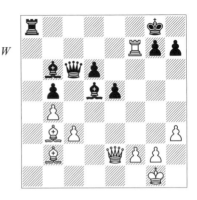

FE45 White to play
(Solution: see page 128)

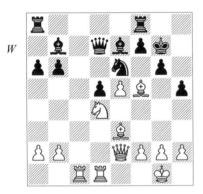

FE44 White to play
(Solution: see page 127)

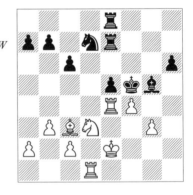

FE46 White to play
(Solution: see page 128)

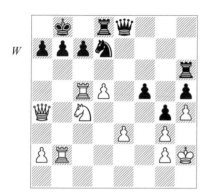

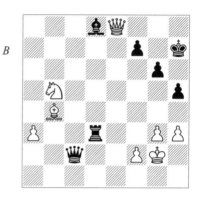

FE47 White to play
(Solution: see page 128)

FE48 Black to play
(Solution: see page 128)

Mixed Bag

As suggested by the title, this section contains a variety of positions, starting with some which could well have been included in the previous 'finger exercises' but moving on to some rather more challenging examples.

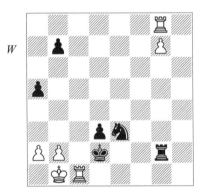

MB01 White to play

The d3-pawn appears to provide some counterplay but White proved otherwise. How?

(Solution: see page 128)

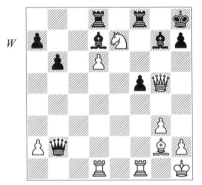

MB02 White to play

(Solution: see page 128)

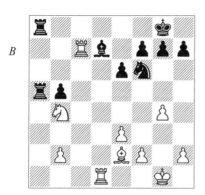

MB03 Black to play

Black challenged the enemy rook with 22...♖8a7 but this was a very bad idea. Why?

(Solution: see page 129)

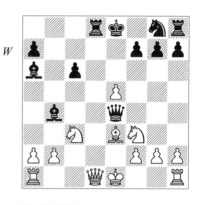

MB05 White to play

(Solution: see page 129)

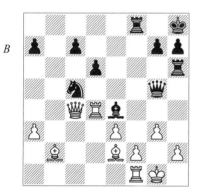

MB04 Black to play

(Solution: see page 129)

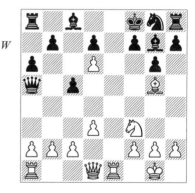

MB06 White to play

Evidently, White has just sacrificed a knight on d6. How did he justify this?

(Solution: see page 129)

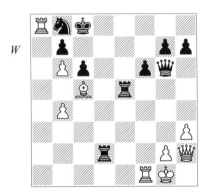

MB07 White to play
How can White break through?
(Solution: see page 129)

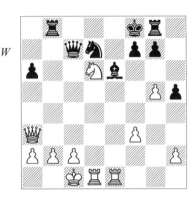

MB09 White to play
What is the cleanest win?
(Solution: see page 129)

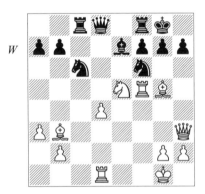

MB08 White to play
(Solution: see page 129)

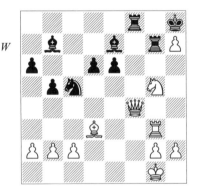

MB10 White to play
(Solution: see page 130)

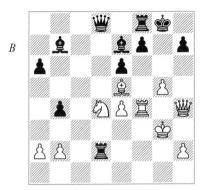

MB11 Black to play

Black chose 33...♕xd4, thinking that after its capture the attack would be broken and he would win on material. Why was this not a good idea?

(Solution: see page 130)

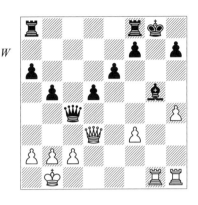

MB13 White to play

White opted for 22 ♕e3, which was apparently a good idea since it 'increased his options'. However, this was an illusion. Why?

(Solution: see page 130)

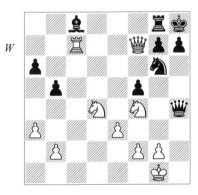

MB12 White to play

What is the cleanest way to win?

(Solution: see page 130)

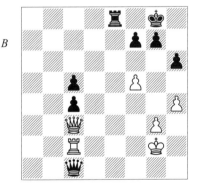

MB14 Black to play

(Solution: see page 130)

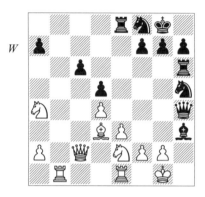

MB15 White to play

White tried to bail out with 20 &f5 but got no joy. Why?

(Solution: see page 130)

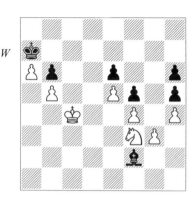

MB17 White to play

If 59 ♘d4?? the pawn ending is drawn. White can win slowly with 59 ♔d3 ... but what is the fastest route?

(Solution: see page 130)

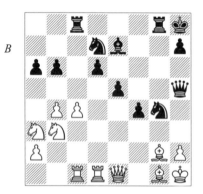

MB16 Black to play

What is the obvious way to continue Black's attack? (White can partially bail out but the resultant position is hopeless.)

(Solution: see page 130)

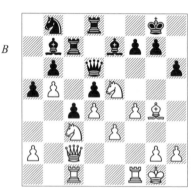

MB18 Black to play

Black played 23...f6 with the laudable aim of driving the knight away, but what was the reply?

(Solution: see page 130)

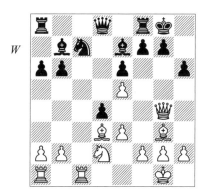

MB19 White to play

White played 17 &f4 in the fond delusion that after 17...dxe3 18 &xh6 g6 19 &xg6 the game would soon be over. What had he missed?

(Solution: see page 131)

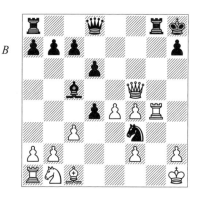

MB21 Black to play
What is the cleanest way?
(Solution: see page 131)

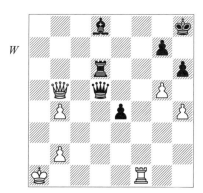

MB20 White to play
(Solution: see page 131)

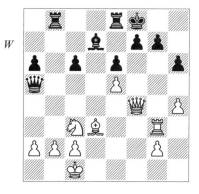

MB22 White to play
(Solution: see page 131)

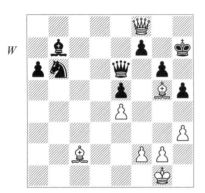

MB23 White to play
How did White force victory?
(Solution: see page 131)

MB25 White to play
The last move was 22...♖f3x♘c3+
(22...♕h7 was also interesting, which
is why I started here).

a) What happens after 23 ♔b1?

b) What is the main line after 23
bxc3 (leading to a better ending)?
(Solution: see page 132)

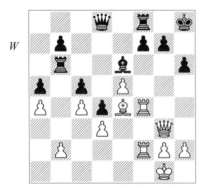

MB24 White to play
White's attack seems temporarily
to have halted. 27 ♖f6 is interesting
but he found a beautiful liquidation.
What was it?

(Solution: see page 131)

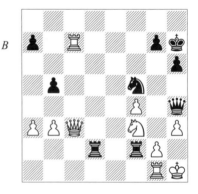

MB26 Black to play
Black chose 37...♕xf4 and soon
won, but there was a much more elegant win. What was it?

(Solution: see page 132)

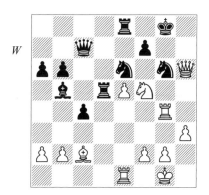

MB27 White to play
What is the cleanest win?
(Solution: see page 132)

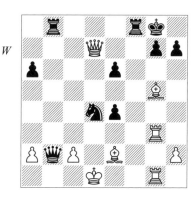

MB29 White to play
(Solution: see page 132)

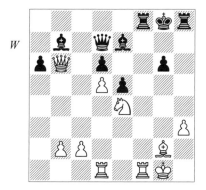

MB28 White to play
(Solution: see page 132)

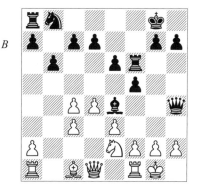

MB30 Black to play
What is the winning line and can
you also see two false trails?
(Solution: see page 132)

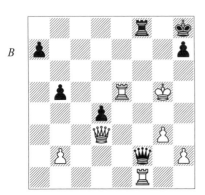

MB31 Black to play
(Solution: see page 132)

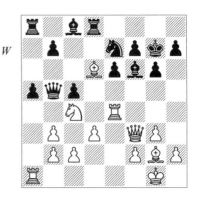

MB33 White to play
(Solution: see page 133)

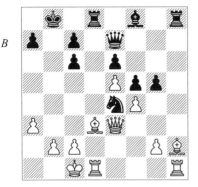

MB32 Black to play

a) Black started with 1...♖xh2. How did he then force a somewhat better ending with a combination which resembled draughts more than chess?

b) Can you see something prosaic and even stronger?

(Solution: see page 133)

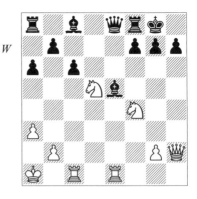

MB34 White to play

What is the main line of the combination and how could Black try to bail out?

(Solution: see page 133)

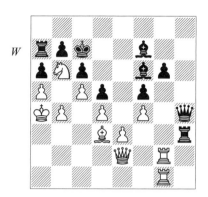

MB35 White to play

White now continued with an impressive combination: 43 ℤxg6 ♗xg6 44 ℤxg6 ℤh2 45 ℤxf6 ℤxe2 46 ℤf8 and after 46...ℤa2+, 47 ♔b3 ♛f2 48 ℤc8# was checkmate. Very nice, but could Black have improved?

(Solution: see page 133)

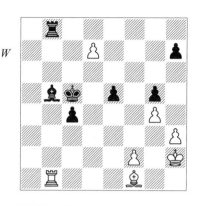

MB37 White to play
(Solution: see page 134)

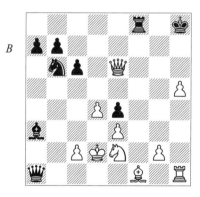

MB36 Black to play
(Solution: see page 133)

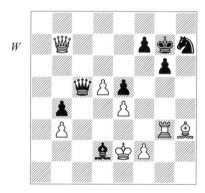

MB38 White to play
This looks difficult since his king is exposed but White found a nice way to prove otherwise. What was it?

(Solution: see page 134)

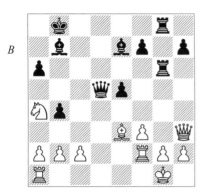

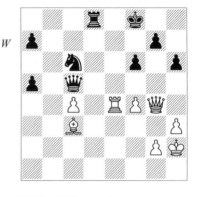

MB39 Black to play

Almost all of Black's pieces are aimed at a single intersection point ...

a) ... which is?

b) How did he intensify the attack with a deflection sacrifice, and what happened when White incautiously took it?

(Solution: see page 134)

MB41 White to play

Despite the limited material and centralized black pieces, White now unleashed a series of blows which proved completely fatal. What were they?

(Solution: see page 134)

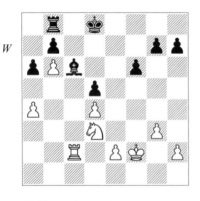

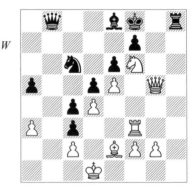

MB40 White to play

In this vastly superior ending, White found a quick kill. What was it?

(Solution: see page 134)

MB42 White to play

Can White bail out?

(Solution: see page 134)

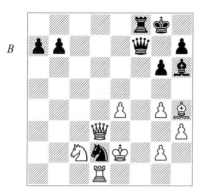

MB43 Black to play
Can Black capture on e4?
(Solution: see page 134)

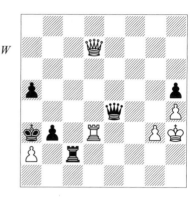

MB45 White to play
(Solution: see page 135)

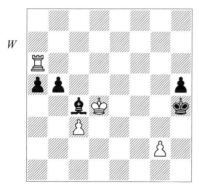

MB44 White to play
(Solution: see page 135)

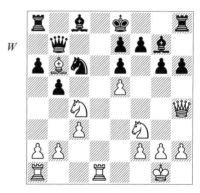

MB46 White to play
Black seems adequately protected
but a nice sequence proved otherwise.
What was it?
(Solution: see page 135)

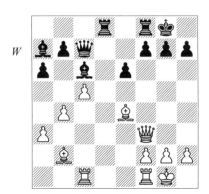

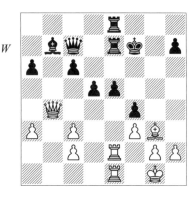

MB47 White to play
(Solution: see page 135)

MB48 White to play
What move does White want to
make, and does it work?
(Solution: see page 135)

Tougher Examples

In this final section, we move on to a series of harder examples, starting with quite soluble ones but moving by the end towards some pretty difficult ones.

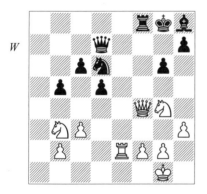

TE01 White to play
(Solution: see page 136)

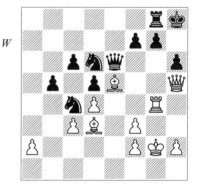

TE02 White to play
After 36 ♖g6 Black resigned. Was this premature?
(Solution: see page 136)

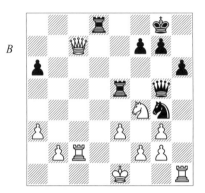

TE03 Black to play

There is a fairly obvious sacrifice but does it work?

(Solution: see page 136)

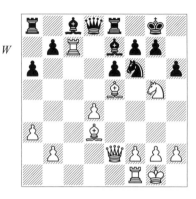

TE05 White to play

(Solution: see page 136)

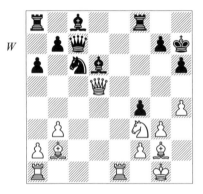

TE04 White to play

(Solution: see page 136)

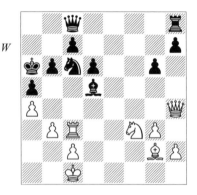

TE06 White to play

(Solution: see page 136)

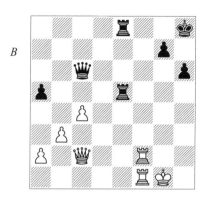

TE07 Black to play

After 1...♖g5+ 2 ♖g2 ♕c5+ 3 ♕f2 White was defending desperately but a single blow finished him off. What was it?

(Solution: see page 136)

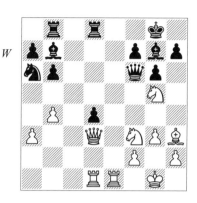

TE09 White to play

How can White use his g5-knight to attack on the light squares?

(Solution: see page 137)

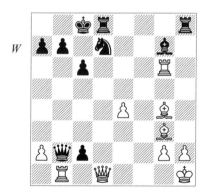

TE08 White to play
(Solution: see page 137)

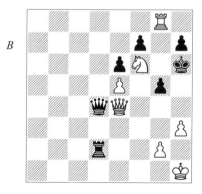

TE10 Black to play
(Solution: see page 137)

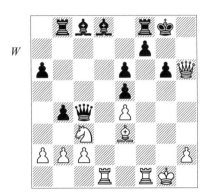

TE11 White to play
(Solution: see page 137)

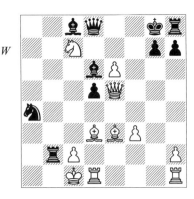

TE13 White to play
(Solution: see page 138)

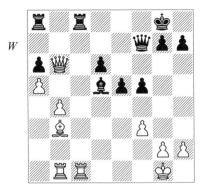

TE12 White to play
White found the beautiful 30 ♕xa6
and Black replied 30...♖xc1+ 31 ♖xc1
♖xa6.

a) What followed?
b) Can you improve for Black?
(Solution: see page 137)

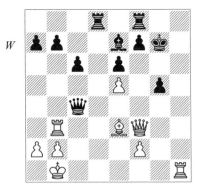

TE14 White to play
(Solution: see page 138)

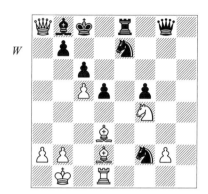

TE15 White to play
(Solution: see page 138)

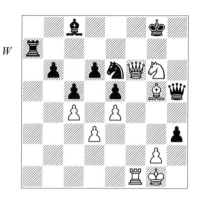

TE17 White to play
(Solution: see page 138)

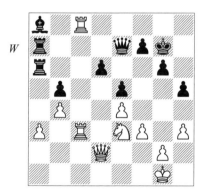

TE16 White to play
(Solution: see page 138)

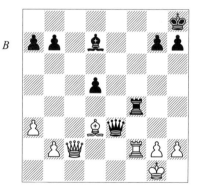

TE18 Black to play
What is the cleanest way to win?
(Solution: see page 138)

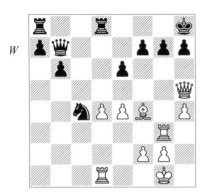

TE19 White to play

What is the obvious sacrifice and can you justify it against best defence?

(Solution: see page 139)

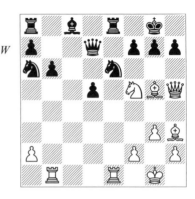

TE21 White to play

How can White attack the enemy king via the dark squares? Please supply just the first two moves and then suggest how White might augment the attack.

(Solution: see page 139)

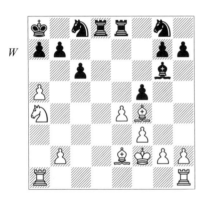

TE20 White to play
(Solution: see page 139)

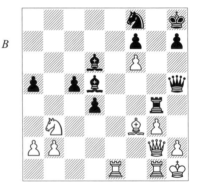

TE22 Black to play

Black's attack seems to have hit a brick wall but he found a brilliant way to continue. How?

(Solution: see page 139)

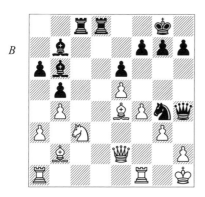

TE23 Black to play

How, nearly a century earlier, did Black set up a finish similar to the previous example?

(Solution: see page 139)

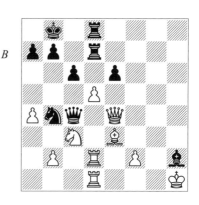

TE25 Black to play

The last two moves played were 27...♗d6x♙h2 28 d4-d5. Obviously, White was trying to bail out, but how did Black now thwart him?

(Solution: see page 140)

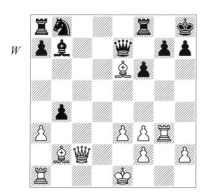

TE24 White to play
(Solution: see page 140)

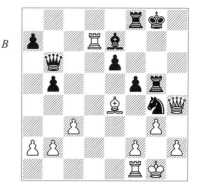

TE26 Black to play

What is Black's best move, and can you see a clear win after the best defence?

(Solution: see page 140)

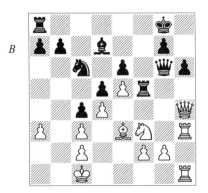

TE27 Black to play
(Solution: see page 140)

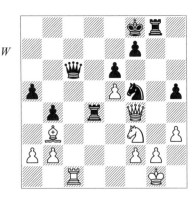

TE29 White to play
With both queens *en prise*, all sorts of ideas are possible. What is White's best move?
(Solution: see page 140)

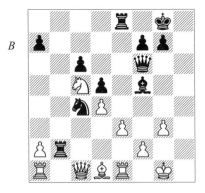

TE28 Black to play
What is Black's best move and what happens if White accepts the bait?
(Solution: see page 140)

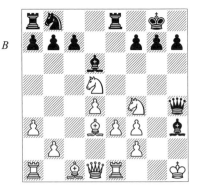

TE30 Black to play
What's the best way for Black to continue the attack and how does he clinch victory if White takes the proffered material?
(Solution: see page 140)

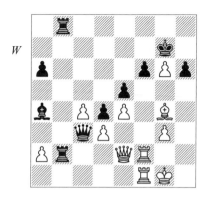

TE31 White to play

In time-trouble White played 31 ♕f3 and eventually drew. But what's the move you want to play, and does it work?

(Solution: see page 141)

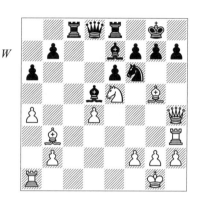

TE33 White to play

White chose 21 ♗d1 *en route* to h5 and won quite quickly. But can you see something even more incisive and its justification?

(Solution: see page 141)

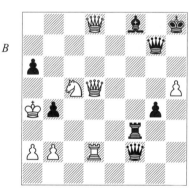

TE32 Black to play
(Solution: see page 141)

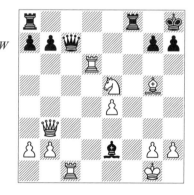

TE34 White to play
(Solution: see page 141)

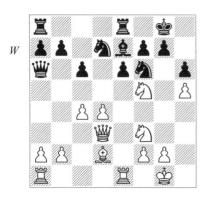

TE35 White to play

White could of course exchange on e7. But there is a much more potent course. What is it and what is the main line if Black takes 'everything'?

(Solution: see page 141)

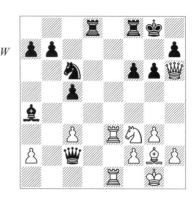

TE37 White to play

How can White break through?

(Solution: see page 142)

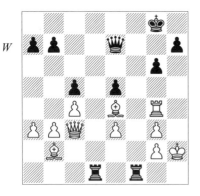

TE36 White to play

What is the best sequence? You can stop after four white moves and three black (at which stage the evaluation of the resultant position isn't at all obvious but seems to be equal).

(Solution: see page 142)

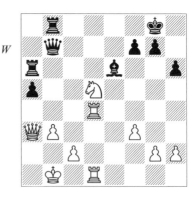

TE38 White to play

(Solution: see page 142)

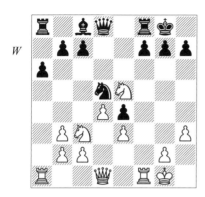

TE39 White to play

What is the main line and can White then coordinate his forces?

(Solution: see page 142)

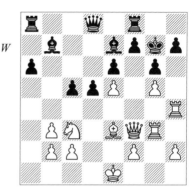

TE41 White to play

(Solution: see page 143)

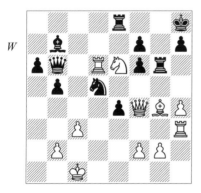

TE40 White to play

What is White's best move and the main line?

(Solution: see page 143)

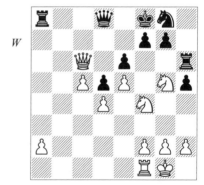

TE42 White to play

Can you find a fabulous win uncovered with computer assistance?

(Solution: see page 143)

Solutions

Knight Forks

KF01

Of course White plays 1 ♘e5+ winning the queen. There are two further points which are worth making though.

If White didn't have the g-pawn then this would only lead to a draw – you have to evaluate the final position of a tactical sequence to decide what the consequences are.

Also, just an apparently slight adjustment of the white pieces would invalidate the 'combination'. If the white king and pawn are switched round then 1 ♘e5+ is impossible since the knight is pinned and Black wins.

KF02

White forces a knight fork next move with a typical deflection: 1 e4+ ♔xe4 (this is much the better way to lose the queen since the king moves towards the kingside; if instead 1...♕xe4, then 2 ♘c3+ ♔d4 3 ♘xe4 ♔xe4 4 ♔g3) 2 ♘g3+ ♔f4 3 ♘xf5 ♔xf5. This is the end of the small combination but again we need to evaluate the consequences. In fact White wins only with 4 ♔h3!, after which he can take the opposition: 4...♔g5 5 ♔g3 and you can find the rest in any endgame book.

Again I reiterate a small change in the initial position would change the final outcome. Had, for instance, the white king started on h1 or the pawn been on h3, then in both cases he final result would have been a draw.

KF03

This is almost identical to KF02 except that it is the bishop which immolates itself for a higher cause: 1 ♗e6+ ♕xe6 (or 1...♔xe6 2 ♘d4+) 2 ♘g5+ ♔f6 3 ♘xe6 ♔xe6 4 ♔g3! ♔f5 5 ♔f3 and wins.

KF04
Galdunts – Steiner
Vienna 2006

23 ♕g4+! won on the spot in view of 23...♕xg4 24 ♘xf6+ and 25 ♘xg4. Note, however, that a different knight fork 23 ♘xd6 was much less effective since after 23...♕g6, 24 ♘xe8?? allows 24...♕xg2#!

KF05
Petrosian – Spassky
World Ch (10), Moscow 1966

In this famous position from a world championship match, Petrosian finished off very prettily with 29 ♗xf7+ ♖xf7 30 ♕h8+! 1-0. After 30...♔xh8 31 ♘xf7+ White will be a piece up.

KF06
Smirin – Pelletier
Biel 2003
28 ♕xe6! won on the spot in view of 28...♖xe6 29 ♘f7+.

KF07
Xie Jun – Short
Jinan 2002
After 51...g4?? 52 ♕h8+ ♔g6 53 ♕xg7+! Black resigned.

KF08
Borosova – Rozić
European Under-18 Girls Ch, Obrenovac 2004
19 ♕h8+! ♔xh8 20 ♘xf7+ ♔g8 21 ♘xg5 completely destroyed Black's pawn-structure and White went on to win.

KF09
Timman – Kosashvili
Curaçao 2002
After 41 ♕xg7+! ♔xg7 42 ♘xh5+ ♔f7 43 ♘xf4 White had an extra outside passed pawn, which is almost always decisive in a knight ending. It finished 43...♔e7 44 h4 ♔d6 45 h5 ♘g4 46 ♔c3 ♘h6 47 a5 ♘g4 48 a6 1-0.

KF10
Miles – Anastasian
European Team Ch, Debrecen 1992
After 28 ♖c8+! Black resigned on the spot on account of 28...♖xc8 (or: 28...♔h7 29 ♘f8+; 28...♔f7 29 ♖8c7) 29 ♖xc8+ ♕xc8 (if 29...♔f7, then 30

♖f8+ ♔xg6 31 ♕d3+ ♔g5 32 ♕g3#) 30 ♘e7+.

KF11
Khuzman – Kasparov
European Clubs Cup, Rethymnon 2003
21 ♖xd5! couldn't be taken either way in view of 21...♕xd5 22 ♘e7+ or 21...♘xd5 22 ♕xg7#. After 21...♕e8 22 ♗xc4 Kasparov resigned immediately in disgust.

KF12
Cekro – Pelletier
European Team Ch, Plovdiv 2003
51 ♘c6! ♕xc8 52 ♘xe7+ ♔f8 53 ♘xc8 won a piece. Since Black has a far-advanced passed pawn, it's important to calculate further here but in fact after 53...b3 54 ♘d2 the pawn is easily stopped and Black resigned.

KF13
Külaots – Tallaksen
Gausdal 2003
36 ♖f3+! ♗xf3 (or 36...♔e7 37 ♘f5+ ♔d8 38 ♖d3+) 37 ♕xf3+ ♔e7 38 ♘f5+ and now 38...♔xe6 is met by 39 ♘xg7+, and 38...♔f6 by 39 ♘d6+. Black played 38...♔d8 but resigned after 39 ♕a8+.

KF14
Bogdanovich – Golubev
Odessa 2004
He could have won material with a combination of deflections and knight forks: 26...♘d2+! 27 ♔f2 (27 ♔g1?

♘xf3+) 27...♗c5+! 28 ♖xc5 (or 28
♔g3 ♗d6) 28...♘e4+ and 29...♘xc5.

KF15
Vlassov – Nakamura
Internet blitz 2004

1 ♕xf7+! annihilated the base of
Black's pawn-chain and after 1...♖xf7
2 ♘xe6+ ♔g8 3 ♘xc5 ♗xh4 4 ♘d3
White had a winning advantage.

KF16
Rowson – McDonald
British Ch, Torquay 2002

The game ended 46...♗b2! 47 ♗b3
♗xc1 48 ♗xc2 ♗xa3 49 b5 ½-½.

46...♗b2 *(D)* was of course the
move I wanted you to find but there
was quite a lot of difficult judgement
bound up in this sequence too.

KF17
Lagowski – Berczes
Budapest 2005

The pin on the knight appears an-
noying and 52...♕xe1 53 ♕xf3+ is
only a draw. However, Black solved
the problem at a single stroke with
52...♕c2+!, when White resigned in
view of 53 ♕xc2 ♘xe1+.

KF18
J. Speelman (end of a study)
8th Comm., Nunn-50JT, 2005

To conclude this chapter, here is the
end of a study of my own, which, given
the nature of the chapter, shouldn't
have presented too much difficulty.

The main line goes 1 ♘d7+ (1
♘xf7? allows stalemate: 1...♕a3+ 2
♔b6 ♕a7+) 1...♕xd7 *(D)*.

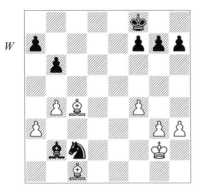

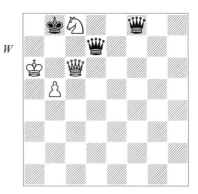

If 47 ♗xb2 ♘e3+ 48 ♔f3 ♘xc4 49
♗c1 f5 50 b5 ♔f7 51 ♔e2 ♔e6 52
♔d3 ♔d5 53 a4 g6 Black is at least
equal, but a move later he correctly
avoided 47...♘a1 48 ♗xb2 ♘xb3, after
which the knight is badly misplaced.

2 ♕a8+ ♔xa8 (White secures a database win after 2...♔c7 3 b6+ ♔d8 4
♘a7+ ♔e7 5 ♘c6+ ♔f7 6 ♘e5+ ♔e6
7 ♕xf8 ♕a4+ 8 ♔b7 ♔xe5 9 ♕c5+
♔f4 10 ♔c7) 3 ♘b6+ ♔b8 4 ♘xd7+
and 5 ♘xf8.

Loose Pieces

LP01
Christiansen – Karpov
Wijk aan Zee 1993

This arose after 1 d4 ♘f6 2 c4 e6 3 ♘f3 b6 4 a3 ♗a6 5 ♕c2 ♗b7 6 ♘c3 c5 7 e4 cxd4 8 ♘xd4 ♘c6 9 ♘xc6 ♗xc6 10 ♗f4 ♘h5 11 ♗e3. Here 11...♗c5 has been played or 11...♕b8 to control f4 but Karpov hit upon a most unfortunate novelty: after 11...♗d6?? 12 ♕d1! White won a whole piece and Black resigned instantly. But Karpov nevertheless levelled the score as White in the next game and went on to win the mini-match against Christiansen in this knockout tournament.

LP02
Adams – M. Gurevich
Turin Olympiad 2006

27...b6 fatally exposed the a8-rook. After 28 ♘xd5! Black resigned on the spot.

LP03
J. Costa – Mladenov
World Under-12 Ch, Oropesa del Mar 1999

With two loose black pieces it's not too surprising that White can win material.

22 ♖e8+! forced the enemy king onto an exposed diagonal preparing a fork two moves later: 22...♔g7 23 ♖e2 ♖b3 (if 23...♖d7 the bishop simply retreats to e3, for example) 24 ♖xb2! ♖xb2 25 ♗d4+ f6 26 ♗xb2 1-0.

LP04
Åkesson – Meijere
Rilton Cup, Stockholm 1998

He continued 25 ♖xc6 ♕xc6 26 ♕d4+ ♗f6 27 ♕xa7 regaining the piece and winning the game a few moves later.

(In fact the more complex 25 ♕c3+ ♔g8 26 ♕xc6 ♕xe4 27 ♖g5+ ♗xg5 28 ♕xe4 ♗xc1 29 ♕g4+ ♔h7 30 ♕f5+ ♔g7 31 ♕c5 is also very strong.)

LP05
Carro – Rossolimo
La Coruña 1951

After 1...♕c1+ 2 ♔h2 ♕f4+ Black wins material since if 3 ♔h1 ♕f1+ the fork wins the exchange, while after 3 ♔g1 ♘f3+ the discovered attack wins queen for knight.

LP06
Karpov – Hübner
Montreal 1979

In time-trouble Karpov played 39 ♕c4 and only drew.

Instead after 39 ♖g8+ ♔h7 *(D)*:

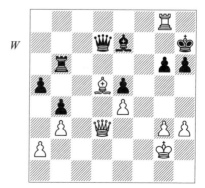

a) 40 ♖xg6 exploits Black's loose queen. If 40...♖xg6, then 41 ♗g8+! or 40...♔xg6 41 ♗f7+! though Black can fight on with 40...♕c7.

b) 40 ♕e3! is even stronger, simultaneously attacking the rook and threatening 41 ♖h8+!. Black then has nothing better than the hopeless 40...♖e6.

LP07
Anand – Kasimdzhanov
FIDE World Cup, Hyderabad 2002

After the deflection 27 d8♕! ♖xd8, 28 ♕a5 put two black pieces *en prise*. 28...♗xe4 29 ♕xd8+ ♗f8 30 f3 ♗f5 and Kasimdzhanov resigned.

LP08
Strating – Van der Schilden
Haarlem 1996

After 11...♖xb2??, 12 ♕xd8+ ♔xd8 13 0-0-0+ won a rook, forcing instant resignation.

This shot, exploiting the castling rules, has occurred a number of times over the years. Of course castling has still to be legal, which is why I emphasized that it was an opening position.

LP09
R. Philipps – Gagnon
Montreal 1998

23...♖xc4! 24 ♖xc4 ♕d5 won a piece and White resigned a few moves later. (I was reminded of this pattern by example LP07 since I once lost exactly this way in a blitz game against Kasimdzhanov.)

LP10
Sadilek – Seknicka
Vienna 2006

This arose after 1 d4 e6 2 e4 d5 3 ♘d2 dxe4 4 ♘xe4 ♘d7 5 ♘f3 ♘gf6 6 ♗g5 ♗e7 7 ♘xf6+ ♗xf6 8 ♗d3 0-0 9 ♕e2 when Black blundered horribly with 9...b6?? 10 ♗xf6 ♗xf6 11 ♕e4! and resigned immediately.

The pattern with ♗d3 and ♕e4 attacking both h7 and a8 is important in the theory of lots of similar lines. Sometimes ...b6 is thus prevented but sometimes, although White temporarily wins a rook, his queen gets into trouble in the corner...

LP11
Ivanchuk – Karpov
Las Palmas 1996

This started 1 e4 e6 2 d4 d5 3 ♘c3 dxe4 4 ♘xe4 ♘d7 5 ♗d3 ♘gf6 6 ♕e2 c5 7 ♘xf6+ ♘xf6 8 dxc5 ♗xc5 9 ♘f3 ♕c7 10 0-0 0-0 11 ♗g5 b6.

Ivanchuk now rather amazingly decided to bail out immediately. After 12 ♘e5 ♗b7 13 ♗xf6 gxf6 14 ♗xh7+ he forced perpetual check so they agreed a draw.

The point I wanted to make though was that after 12 ♗xf6 gxf6 13 ♕e4 f5 14 ♕xa8 ♗b7 15 ♕xa7 (if 15 ♕xf8+ ♔xf8 Black is very active), 15...b5! traps the queen to emerge with a small material advantage. In tactical lines you have to analyse until you believe that the position is quiescent and here it certainly wasn't good enough to stop after 14 ♕xa8.

LP12
Adams – Bareev
Wijk aan Zee 2004

Simply 24 ♕xf6 gxf6 25 ♖xe6! won a vital pawn and Bareev resigned immediately in disgust.

LP13
Mamedyarov – Kharlov
Sochi 2006

After 20 ♘xf7 ♖xf7 21 ♖xe6 ♕d7 the rook appears to be pinned but 22 ♖xf6! ♕xg4 23 ♖xf7! proved otherwise. The threat of a discovered check is now so strong that White wins another piece and after 23...♔h8 24 ♖xe7 ♖c8 25 ♖xc8+ ♕xc8 26 d5 Black resigned.

LP14
Areshchenko – Rogovsky
Ukrainian Ch, Simferopol 2003

After 15 ♕d5+ ♔h8 16 ♕xc5 Black played the highly aesthetic 16...♘g3+! 17 hxg3 ♕h5+ 18 ♔g1 ♘xf3+! 19 gxf3 ♕xc5+, winning the queen and the game a couple of moves later.

LP15
C. Torre – Em. Lasker
Moscow 1925

In this very famous example, White is able to set up a discovered check and then, after capturing a piece, repeatedly reset it, thus creating a so-called 'see-saw'.

After 25 ♗f6! ♕xh5 26 ♖xg7+ ♔h8 27 ♖xf7+ ♔g8 28 ♖g7+ ♔h8 29 ♖xb7+ ♔g8 30 ♖g7+ ♔h8 White

doesn't have an immediate knockout but has won several pawns. Rather than capture on a7 – which would activate the a8-rook – he decided to take the queen at once with 31 ♖g5+ ♔h7 32 ♖xh5. Black was lucky (or perhaps unlucky since it merely prolonged his suffering) to have 32...♔g6 regaining the piece but after 33 ♖h3 ♔xf6 34 ♖xh6+ ♔g5 35 ♖h3 White was three pawns up and soon won.

Opening and Closing Lines

LO01
Makogonov – Flohr
Match (8), Baku 1942

Were the bishop not on d6 blocking the d-file, then ♕d8 would be immediate mate.

41 ♗b8! *(D)* cleared the d-file with tempo.

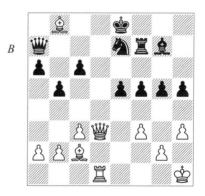

Black resigned immediately in view of 41...♕xb8 42 ♕d7+ ♔f8 43 ♕d8+ ♕xd8 44 ♖xd8# leading to an unusual back-rank mate.

LO02
Zamora – G. Garcia
Cuban Ch, Havana 1965

1...♗d4! unpinned the rook, threatening 2...♖xc3 and thus inducing the line-opening 2 cxd4. After 2...♖xa3 3 ♖e1 (or 3 dxc5 ♖xa1+) 3...♕d5 White resigned. Obviously I could also have included this in the section on pins.

LO03
Alekhine – Hulscher
Simultaneous, Netherlands 1933

Here White's task is to prevent the enemy king from running to f7, which he achieved with 16 ♘e5!! dxe5 (or 16...♕xe5 17 ♕xe5 dxe5 18 g6 and 19 ♖h8#) 17 g6! ♕xg6 18 ♕c4+! and Black resigned.

LO04
Von Popiel – Marco
Monte Carlo 1902

Obviously Black thought that the pin was costing him a piece but 36...♗g1! would have turned the tables – after 37 ♔xg1 ♖xd3 Black is winning.

LO05
Trifunović – Aaron
Beverwijk 1962

This time the bishop isn't pinned but the line-clearance with tempo 31 ♗g8! was again decisive.

This was easy after the last example, but I wanted to emphasize that the same patterns recur in chess games, even if they are slightly unusual.

LO06
Svidler – Bareev
Wijk aan Zee 2004

Here Bareev had just blundered with 16...exf4??. Again the problem was to open a line with tempo – in this case the e-file – and Svidler hit him with the (fairly obvious) 17 ♗xb7!. Now if 17...♕xb7, then 18 ♕d8#; or 17...♗xb7 18 ♖fe1 ♕xe1+ 19 ♖xe1+ ♔f8 20 ♕d7. 17...0-0 18 ♗xa8 ♕a7+ 19 ♕d4 ♕xa8 20 ♖xf4 is also hopeless so Bareev resigned on the spot.

LO07
Fischer – Benko
USA Ch, New York 1963/4

In another very famous example, Black is intending to defend himself with ...f5 but Fischer discovered a brilliant way to prevent this: 19 ♖f6!! *(D)* blocked the f-pawn.

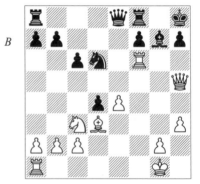

If 19...♗xf6, then 20 e5 forces immediate mate so Benko tried 19...♔g8 instead, but after 20 e5 h6 21 ♘e2 he resigned.

LO08
Réti – Bogoljubow
New York 1924

Although White has an attack it looks as though Black might survive. However, a single beautiful move demonstrated otherwise: 25 ♗e8! cut the back rank and Black resigned immediately in view of 25...♖xe8 26 ♕xf8+ ♖xf8 27 ♖xf8#.

LO09
Ståhlberg – Persitz
Ljubljana 1955

In this analogous position White cut the back rank with 17 ♗b8!. Here it wasn't instantly fatal but after 17...♘e4 (of course if 17...♖axb8?, 18 ♕xb8 ♖xb8 19 ♖xb8+ mates) 18 ♗xe4 ♖axb8 19 ♕xb8 dxe4 20 ♕f4 White had won the exchange and went on to complete victory on move 39.

LO10
Vaganian – T.L. Petrosian
Moscow 2004

Black looks secure enough but the stunning 35 ♗xd5+!! proved otherwise. If 35...cxd5, then 36 ♖a7+ and the two rooks force mate so Black tried 35...♔g7 but after 36 ♗b3 ♖b4 (36...♖dxd4 37 ♗xa4 ♖xa4 38 ♖b7+ ♗xb7 39 ♖xa4) 37 ♖xa6 ♖d3 38 ♖a3 ♖b7 39 ♔e2 ♖xd4 40 ♖ba2 he resigned.

LO11
Kasperovich – Bukhman
USSR 1977

Here Black wants to get his queen to g1 but can't play 1...♕g1? immediately in view of 2 ♖g2+.

1...♖g6! solved Black's problem: 2 ♗xg6 ♕g1 3 ♗xf7+ ♔h7! 4 ♗g6+ ♔h6! and White resigned.

LO12
Yusupov – Lobron
Nussloch 1996

White had let rip the previous move with the highly thematic 19 d5!, which was met by 19...♘c6-a5 (if 19...exd5, 20 ♖xe7! wins but 19...♘xd5 is more complicated). Now everything points to 20 dxe6!! *(D)*, releasing all the energy in the white position, and indeed it does work:

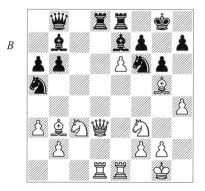

a) If 20...♖xd3 21 exf7+ ♔g7 22 fxe8♕ ♕xe8 23 ♖xd3 ♘xb3 24 ♖de3 ♔f7 White has lots of good lines. Simply 25 ♖xe7+ ♕xe7 26 ♖xe7+ ♔xe7 27 ♘e5 ♔e6 28 ♗xf6 ♔xf6 29 ♘d7+ is quite good enough.

b) Black therefore tried 20...♘xb3 but 21 exf7+ ♔xf7 22 ♕c4+ ♔g7 23

♘e5! was crushing and the game ended 23...♘g8 24 ♖xd8 ♕xd8 25 ♕f7+ ♔h8 26 ♕xb3 ♕d4 27 ♖e3! ♖f8 28 ♗xe7 1-0.

LO13
Rublevsky – Klimov
Russian Ch, Krasnoiarsk 2003

Black's attempt to defend through a back-rank trick (28 ♖xf5?? ♖d1+) was thwarted by 28 ♘xe6+! ♕xe6 29 ♖xg7, when the triple attack on f7 was utterly fatal and after 29...♖d7 30 ♕g8+ he resigned.

LO14
Karpov – Topalov
Dos Hermanas 1994

30 ♘f6!! introduced a beautiful, highly geometrical combination. After 30...♔xf6 (30...♕xf3 31 ♘xe8+) 31 ♗e5++! ♔xe5 32 ♕xe4+ ♔xe4 33 ♖e1+ ♔f5 34 ♖xe8 the fork regained a piece, leaving Karpov the exchange ahead. Topalov resigned after 34...♗e6 35 ♖xf8 ♗xa2 36 ♖c8.

LO15
H. Rinck
Deutsche Schachzeitung, 1906

In this short but pretty study White wins by means of a problem theme known as a Novotny, whereby a piece is sacrificed on a square where it can be taken by either of two different enemy units – but whichever one makes the capture, it interferes with the other.

1 a7 ♗g2 2 d7 ♖d2 3 ♗d5! forces the promotion of one or other of the pawns. Black's best defence is 3...♖xd5 but after 4 a8♕ ♖xd7 5 ♕f8+ ♔g6 6 ♕e8+ ♖f7 7 ♕e6+ ♖f6 8 ♕g4+ ♔f7 9 ♕g8+ (9 ♕xg2?? ♖h6#) 9...♔e7 10 ♕xg2 White reaches the won ending of queen vs rook.

Pins

PI01

Of course White wins with 1 ♗e5, creating an absolute pin of the knight against the king. After 1...♔g7 either 2 h4 or 2 f4 prevents Black from unpinning by ...g5 and ...♔g6 and in fact puts Black into immediate zugzwang.

a) If the pawn starts on h6 then 1 ♗e5 ♔g7 2 h4! still wins after 2...g5 3 h5! – but now 2 f4 doesn't work.

PI02
Radziewicz – Khamrakulova
World Girls Ch, Athens 2001

33 ♖cxe6 ♖xe6 34 ♗xd5 not only fatally pins the e6-rook but also skewers the two black rooks. After 34...♔g7 35 ♗xe6 ♖a5 36 ♗h4 Black resigned.

PI03
Speelman – M. Piket
Dordrecht (blitz) 2003

1 ♖c7 ♖d7 2 ♕xf7+! ♖xf7 3 ♖xd7 forced resignation.

PI04
Golubev – Mantovani
Biel 1992

After 26 ♕xc5+! the main point is that if 26...♕xc5, then 27 ♘c6+ ♔a8

28 ♖xb8#. Black tried 26...♕b6 but resigned after 27 ♘c6+ ♔a8 28 ♖xb6.

PI05
Radjabov – Dao Thien Hai
Turin Olympiad 2006
After 36...g6? 37 hxg6 ♕xg6+ 38 ♖g4! Black resigned.

PI06
Vidarsson – Stefansson
Icelandic Ch, Seltjarnarnes 2002
28...♗c3! *(D)* utilized the pin along the second rank, forcing instant resignation in view of the threat of 29...♖d2.

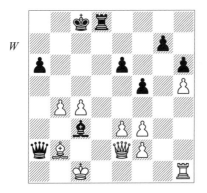

If 29 ♖d1, then 29...♗xb2+, or 29 ♕c2 ♗d2+ 30 ♔d1 ♗xe3+ 31 ♔e1 ♖d2.

PI07
This opening catastrophe, which arises after 1 e4 e5 2 ♘f3 ♘c6 3 ♗c4 h6? 4 d4 d6 5 ♘c3 ♗g4 6 dxe5 ♘xe5? was first described (actually in a slightly different form) by Legall de Kermeur (1702-92), the champion of the Café de la Régence and Philidor's teacher. It has occurred a number of times over the years and indeed I found three different games in a large database. The pin is only relative, and White wins with 7 ♘xe5! ♗xd1 8 ♗xf7+ ♔e7 9 ♘d5#.

PI08
Renet – Miles
Linares Zonal 1995
...and many other games.
This arises after 1 e4 ♘c6 2 ♘f3 d6 3 d4 ♘f6 4 ♘c3 ♗g4 5 d5. It turns out that 5...♘e5 is quite playable since after 6 ♘xe5 ♗xd1 7 ♗b5+ c6 8 dxc6 dxe5! 9 c7+ (if 9 cxb7+?, then 9...♘d7!) 9...♕d7 10 ♗xd7+ ♔xd7 11 ♔xd1 Black can play either 11...♔xc7 or 11...e6 (as chosen in the game) first.
It's important to remember that tactical sequences like this depend on the exact position. After 1 e4 ♘c6 2 ♘f3 d6 3 d4 ♗g4 4 d5 ♘e5 (i.e. with knights on b1 and g8) 5 ♘xe5 ♗xd1 6 ♗b5+ c6 7 dxc6, 7...♕a5+ 8 ♘c3 0-0-0 is complicated though 9 ♘c4 seems to be good for White; but what is absolutely clear is that 7...dxe5? loses outright to 8 cxb7+.

PI09
Mohandesi – Barsov
Leuven 2002
Black was able to unpin by playing 13...♘xe4! 14 ♗xd8 (14 ♘xe4 ♕xh4+ is hopeless for White) 14...♘xf3+! 15 ♔f1 (if 15 gxf3, then 15...♗f2+ 16 ♔f1 ♗h3#) 15...♘ed2+! 16 ♕xd2

♘xd2+ 17 ♔e1 ♘xb1 and White resigned half a dozen moves later.

PI10
Flohr – Bronstein
Pärnu 1947
If 20...♘cxd5 21 ♘exd5 ♘xd5 22 ♗xg7 ♕xg7 23 ♘xd5 ♕d4+ 24 ♔h1 ♕xd5, 25 ♗c4! is a sting in the tail. After 25...♕xc4 26 ♖xc4 bxc4 27 ♕d5+ White has excellent winning chances.

PI11
A. Troitsky
L'Echiquier, 1930
In this nice study White twice uses the pin to good effect – the first instance being a 'cross-pin'. 1 ♕f6+ ♔h5 2 ♕f5+ ♔h6 3 ♗e3+ ♔g7 4 ♕g5+ ♔f8 5 ♗c5+ ♗d6 6 ♕e5! ♕d8 7 ♗xd6+ ♔g8 8 ♕g3+ ♔h8 9 ♗e5+ f6 10 ♕g5!.

PI12
After 1...♖a1+ 2 ♔h2 ♕g1+ 3 ♔g3 ♖a3+ 4 ♖d3 White seems to be escaping unscathed but 4...♕d4! proves otherwise.

PI13
Onescius – Gama
Romanian Ch, Bucharest 1955
After 1 ♘xf3 exf3! the deflection 2 ♕g7+!! defends. 2...♔xg7 (2...♖xg7 3 ♖e8+ ♖g8 4 ♖xg8+ ♔xg8 5 gxh4 is worse) 3 gxh4 and White has a decisive advantage though he must still be careful; for example, if 3...♔h8+ 4 ♔h1 ♖xh4 5 ♖g1 (but not 5 ♖xd5?

♖g2) 5...♖xg1+ 6 ♔xg1 ♘f4 and now perhaps 7 ♗c8.

PI14
Toran – Kuijpers
Malaga 1965
23...♗d4+ 24 ♗e3 ♕g5?? 25 ♕xd4! and Black resigned.

PI15
Olsen – Jakobsen
Århus 1953
1 ♖exd5?? ♕xg2+!! 2 ♔xg2 ♗xc6 and it was White who had to resign.

Skewers

SK01
In this, one of the fundamental positions of rook endings, White wins with 1 ♖h8! ♖xa7 (Black can check first but it doesn't in any way help him) 2 ♖h7+.

SK02
Hebden – Speelman
Southend 2000
This is a good example of why the basic patterns are important in practical play. Here I'd just blundered with 1...♔f7-e7?? – 1...♖a5 first would have drawn.

After 2 a7! ♖a5 3 ♖h6! I resigned since there's no defence to the threat of 4 ♖h8! ♖xa7 5 ♖h7+.

SK03
L. van Vliet
Deutsche Schachzeitung, 1888

This theoretical ending features a variety of skewers after the black queen has been deflected.

If 1...♕d5, then 2 ♕a4+ ♔b6 3 ♕b3+!; 1...♕f3 2 ♕a4+ ♔b6 3 ♕b3+! or 1...♕g2 2 ♕a3+ ♔b6 3 ♕b2+!. 1...♕h1 is the most stubborn, when after 2 ♕a3+ ♔b6 3 ♕b2+, both 3...♔a5 4 ♕a2+ ♔b4 5 ♕b1+ and 3...♔c7 4 ♕h2+ also lead to skewers, while 3...♔c5 4 ♔a7 ♕h7 5 ♕b6+ ♔c4 6 ♔a6 is also winning for White.

SK04

In this very simple example position, 1 f3+! deflects the queen and after 1...♕xf3, 2 ♕a8+ wins it.

SK05

P. Schlosser – Raetsky
Cappelle la Grande 2003

If White takes the rook, Black will give perpetual check but White is able to win the enemy queen with a typical sequence: 49 ♕f8+ ♔h7 50 ♘f6+ ♔g6 51 ♕g8+! and Black resigned in view of 51...♔xf6 52 ♕h8+.

SK06

Bocharov – Nayer
Tomsk 2006

Black finished off with 64...♕g6+ 65 ♔h3 (if 65 ♔f3 still 65...h1♕) 65...h1♕+ 66 ♕xh1 ♕h6+ and Black resigned in view of 67 ♔g2 ♕xc6+.

SK07

Ionov – Zhelnin
USSR 1980

White broke through with 1 ♖xg5 ♘xg5 2 ♗xf6 gxf6 (2...♘f7 3 ♕h7+ ♔f8 4 ♕xg7+ ♔e8 5 ♕g8+) 3 ♕h8+ ♔f7 4 ♖h7+! ♘xh7 5 ♕xh7+ and Black resigned.

SK08

Hjelm – Asauskas
Oslo 2003

If 27...♕c7 28 ♖xf7 ♕xd7 29 ♖xd7 White is much better.

But Black was able to force an immediate draw with 27...♕xc1+! 28 ♔xc1 ♖xc2+ 29 ♔d1 ♖c1+ *(D)*.

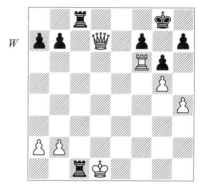

There is no way to escape perpetual check since after 30 ♔e2 ♖8c2+ 31 ♔f3 ♖f1+ 32 ♔e3 ♖e1+ White can't play 33 ♔d3 in view of the skewer 33...♖d1+. Instead after 33 ♔f3 the draw was agreed.

SK09

Alekseev – Aseev
St Petersburg 2000

White played 31 e6? and eventually drew.

He missed a very nice combination with two deflections leading to a skewer: 31 ♘e6! ♖xe6 32 ♖f7! ♔xf7 33 ♕xh7+ ♔e8 34 ♕g8+.

SK10
H. Rinck
Deutsche Schachzeitung, 1905

Skewers often occur in studies. Here in one of numerous similar examples, Henri Rinck demonstrates how the king can be harried onto a fatal square: 1 ♕f1+ ♔d5 (1...♔b3 2 ♕b5+ ♔c2 {or 2...♔a3 3 ♕a5+ ♔b3 4 ♕a2#} 3 ♕b1#) 2 ♘f6+! exf6 3 ♕b5+ ♔e4 4 ♕e2+ ♔f5 5 ♕c2+ ♔g5 (or 5...♔e6 6 ♕b3+) 6 ♕g2+.

SK11
J. Sehwers
Rigaer Tageblatt, 1900

1 ♖a5+ and then:

a) 1...b5 2 ♖xb5+ ♕xb5 (2...♔c6 3 ♗a4 ♕c7 4 b4!) 3 c4+ ♕xc4 (3...♔xc4 4 ♗e2+) 4 ♗b3.

b) The main line goes 1...♔e4 2 ♖f5!! and whichever way Black captures on f5, the queen is lost due to a skewer.

SK12
J. Fritz
Svobodne Slovo, 1953

In this rather harder example, forced play again leads to a skewer: 1 ♘c1+ ♔c2 2 ♘xb3 ♗h4 3 ♘d4+ ♔d3 4 ♘g8! (the hardest move of the solution, which crucially covers f6 and e7) 4...♔xd4 5 ♔g4 ♗f2 6 ♗b6+.

Overloaded Pieces and Deflections

OL01
Svidler – Almasi
Bundesliga 2003/4

The black queen performs a crucial role, defending the rook on e8.

17 ♕g4! deflected the queen and forced instant resignation since of course 17...♕xg4 allows 18 ♖xe8#, while if 17...♘e6 simply 18 ♘xe6.

OL02
Romanishin – Plaskett
London 1977

The black queen has to defend both f6 and d7.

1 ♖xd7! was terminal as 1...♕xd7 2 ♗xf6 ♕d1+ 3 ♗f1 leads to mate; or 1...♘xd7 2 ♕xg7# is immediate mate.

OL03
Van Wely – L'Ami
Dutch Ch, Leeuwarden 2004

Here the white queen has to cover both a2 and c2. 26...♘a2+! deflected the queen, and won on the spot in view of 27 ♕xa2 ♕c2#.

OL04
Esplana – Belli
Peruvian Ch, Lima 2000

Here the black queen performs the crucial task of defending g6.

After 29 ♗d5 Black resigned in view of 29...♕xd5 30 ♕xg6+ ♔f8 when almost anything wins – 31 ♘xf5 or 31 ♕xh7 looks most clinical.

OL05
Marinković – Makarychev
Belgrade 1988

Here two crucial diagonals intersect at d4 and the d1-rook has the vital task of defending the bishop on that square. 23...♖b1! forced resignation since after 24 ♖xb1 ♗xd4+ the fork wins the a7-rook, leaving Black a whole piece up.

OL06
Leko – Grishchuk
Cap d'Agde (rapid) 2003

The g-pawn performs two crucial roles here, defending against the knight fork on h4 and keeping the g-file closed. 36...♘h4+! won on the spot since after 37 gxh4 it has abandoned the latter role and 37...♖g8+ wins the queen.

OL07
Zhao Jun – Minasian
Aeroflot Open, Moscow 2004

After 26 c3? (26 ♔f1 was quite playable) the very pretty 26...♖e8!! forced immediate resignation since after 27 ♕xe8 (or 27 ♕d2 ♗xf2+! 28 ♕xf2 ♖e1+) 27...♗xf2+ 28 ♔h1 ♘g3+ 29 ♔h2 ♗g1+ 30 ♔xg3 ♕f2+ 31 ♔g4 it's mate in two (in three different ways).

OL08
Alcazar Jimenez – Mamedyarov
World Under-18 Ch, Khalkidhiki 2003

35...♕e1+! deflected the queen from the defence of the c2-rook. After 36

♕xe1 ♖xc2 both the queen and mate on h2 were threatened. White tried 37 ♗f5+ ♔f6 but then resigned.

OL09
Leko – Anand
Cap d'Agde (rapid) 2003

37...♘g3+! is obvious since it annihilates the white king's remaining scrap of pawn-cover. It works because after 38 hxg3 ♕h3+ 39 ♔g1 ♕xg3+ 40 ♔h1 Black has 40...♖h4+ deflecting the knight and exploiting the fact – a far from obvious weakness – that the queen is loose. After 41 ♘xh4 ♕xe3 42 ♘g2 ♕e2 43 ♖f5 ♕xb2 44 ♖c5 ♕xa2 45 ♖xc6 a5 Leko resigned.

OL10
Speelman – Velimirović
Maribor 1980

This was from the tournament way back in 1980 where I became a grandmaster. Under slight pressure I was able to bail out with 25 ♗xg7!, when we agreed a draw immediately in view of 25...♘xg7 26 ♘h6+ ♔h8 27 ♘xf7+ with perpetual check, while if 25...♔xg7? 26 ♘e7+ ♔f8 27 ♘xc8 ♗xb2 28 ♘b6 c3 29 ♘c4 c2 30 ♘xb2 cxd1♕+ 31 ♘xd1 White has the advantage.

OL11
A.N. Panchenko – Kochiev
Riga (Under-18) 1973

If 25...♘f5 26 ♕xh7+ ♔f8 27 ♕h8+ ♔e7 28 ♕f6+ White has perpetual check but the excellent 25...♗g4+!

deflected the rook to g4 and after 26 ♖xg4 ♘f5 27 ♕h3 (27 ♕xh7+ doesn't work now because the knight covers h4) 27...♖xc2+ 28 ♔f1 ♕b5+ White resigned.

OL12
Alekhine – NN
Simultaneous, Trinidad 1939
After 1 ♖c8! ♖xc8 the splendid deflection 2 ♕e7!! concluded matters.

OL13
Paglilla – Carbone
Argentina 1985
Of course White can't take the queen due to his weak back rank and if the rook moves away or exchanges then f6 will fall. He solved the problem with one very beautiful and mighty blow: 1 ♕a8!! and Black resigned due to 1...♖xa8 2 fxe7 followed by ♖d8+.

OL14
Malakhov – P.H. Nielsen
European Ch, Istanbul 2003
25 ♘b5! moved the knight out of the way with tempo and after 25...cxb5, 26 ♕f4! overloaded the black queen. Now 26...♕d7 27 ♗xb6 ♕xd4 (or 27...axb6 28 ♖xd7 ♗xd7 29 e5) 28 ♗xd4 ♖xd4 29 ♕e5 is hopeless so Black resigned immediately.

OL15
A. Wotawa
Schach-Magazin, 1951
In this position from the end of a study, White has to find the quickest

way to disturb the enemy bishop. It is: 1 ♗g3 a4 2 ♗h4! (deflection) 2...♗xh4 3 g4+! driving the king to g5 where, however, it cuts the diagonal, allowing 4 d8♕+.

OL16
Maroczy – Bogoljubow
New York 1924
Black played 25...♖e2?! and in fact won very quickly after 26 ♖f1?? ♕xd4+ 27 ♔h1 ♕f6 0-1. However, by 26 ♖xe2 dxe2 27 ♕xf6 e1♕+ 28 ♕f1 ♕e3+ 29 ♕f2 ♕g5+ 30 ♕g3 ♕xg3+ 31 hxg3 White should hold easily even though Black can win the g6-pawn.

Instead 25...♖c1! 26 ♗xc1 (not 26 ♕xf6 ♖xe1+ 27 ♕f1 d2!) 26...♕xf5 27 ♖e8+ ♕f8 28 ♖xf8+ ♔xf8 reaches the same ending but with an extra black pawn on d3, which obviously improves his winning chances.

OL17
Chatalbashev – Cornette
Calvi 2004
At the moment the white king can run to d2 but the excellent 23...♖c2! covered the flight-square. If 24 ♘xc2 the deflection of the knight has opened more of the d-file and 24...♗h3+ 25 ♔f2 ♕g2+ 26 ♔e1 ♕f1# is mate, while 24 ♖e8+ ♔h7 doesn't help. White therefore tried 24 ♕f4 but after 24...♗xe2+ 25 ♔f2 ♗c4+! 26 ♘xc2 (or 26 ♖d2 ♕h2+) the knight had been deflected anyway and he resigned after 26...♕h2+, not waiting for 27 ♔e1 ♕g1#.

OL18
Cyborowski – Mista
Polish Ch, Warsaw 2004

The far from obvious 26 ♗b5! deflected the queen and set up a pyrotechnic finish: 26...♕xb5 27 ♖xg6! fxg6 28 ♕xh5+! gxh5 29 ♖g7#.

Mating Attacks

MA01

The game started 1 e4 g6 2 d4 ♗g7 3 ♘f3 d6 4 ♗c4 and Black has just played the catastrophic 4...♘d7?? *(D)*, fatally weakening the light squares e6 and f7.

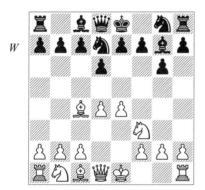

After 5 ♗xf7+! he has resigned in a number of games in view of 5...♔xf7 6 ♘g5+ ♔f8/e8 (of course it's important to check that 6...♔f6 isn't possible but in this case that seems most unlikely and indeed 7 ♕f3# provides a comprehensive answer to the contrary) 7 ♘e6(+) winning the queen. Black has also sometimes struggled on after 5...♔f8 6 ♘g5.

MA02
Sutovsky – Azmaiparashvili
Moscow (rapid) 2002

This features another catastrophe on f7, unusually with a very strong player on the receiving end.

After 24 ♗xf7+ Black resigned immediately in view of 24...♔xf7 25 ♕b3+ ♔e8 (25...♔f8 26 ♘xg6+ ♔e8 27 ♕e6+ or 25...♔f6 26 ♕e6#) 26 ♕e6+ ♔f8 27 ♘xg6#.

MA03
Suba – Sax
Hastings 1983/4

The weakness of f7 also proved fatal here though for a different reason – the knight was deflected from the defence of c6.

The game had gone 1 c4 ♘f6 2 ♘f3 c5 3 ♘c3 d5 4 cxd5 ♘xd5 5 e4 ♘b4 6 ♗c4 ♘d3+ 7 ♔e2 ♘f4+ 8 ♔f1 ♘e6 9 ♘e5 ♕d6 10 f4 ♘c6 11 ♕a4 ♘ed8 12 d4 cxd4 13 ♘b5 ♕b8 14 ♘xd4 f6 15 ♘dxc6 bxc6? and after 16 ♗f7+! Black resigned immediately since 16...♘xf7 17 ♕xc6+ ♔d8 18 ♘xf7# is checkmate.

MA04
Morphy – The Duke of Brunswick and Count Isouard
Paris 1858

This is the finish to one of the most famous games of all time, played, allegedly, in the interval at the opera – so that Morphy wanted to win quickly in order to concentrate on the second half.

The preceding moves were 1 e4 e5 2 ♘f3 d6 3 d4 ♗g4 4 dxe5 ♗xf3 5 ♕xf3 dxe5 6 ♗c4 ♘f6 7 ♕b3 ♕e7 8 ♘c3 c6 9 ♗g5 b5 10 ♘xb5 cxb5 11 ♗xb5+ ♘bd7 12 0-0-0 ♖d8 13 ♖xd7 ♖xd7 14 ♖d1 ♕e6 and Morphy now wrapped things up with 15 ♗xd7+! ♘xd7 16 ♕b8+! ♘xb8 17 ♖d8# (1-0).

MA05
Réti – Tartakower
Vienna (offhand game) 1910

This is another very famous short game in which the king perishes due to the open central files. White forced mate with 9 ♕d8+! ♔xd8 10 ♗g5++ ♔c7 (or 10...♔e8 11 ♖d8#) 11 ♗d8#.

(The opening was 1 e4 c6 2 d4 d5 3 ♘c3 dxe4 4 ♘xe4 ♘f6 5 ♕d3 e5? 6 dxe5 ♕a5+ 7 ♗d2 ♕xe5 8 0-0-0 ♘xe4?.)

MA06
Ostropolsky – Ivanovsky
USSR 1949

This features the same pattern as in the previous examples but quite well disguised: 1 ♕xd7+! ♖xd7 2 ♘c7+ ♖xc7 3 ♖d8#.

MA07
a) 1...♕h3 is met by 2 ♕h8+! ♔xh8 3 ♘xg6++ ♔g8 4 ♘e7#.

b) 1...♕e6 is slightly different: 2 ♕h8+! ♔xh8 3 ♘xf7++ ♔g8 4 ♘h6#.

The knight has to change its route depending on whether the black queen defends h6 or e7. Note the pawn which I added on a7 to prevent 1...♕a7+

though in fact even then 2 ♔h1 ♖xb2 3 ♘c6 wins.

MA08
Cramer – Zilverberg
Leeuwarden 1992

In this simple example from a real game, Black had just played 15...♗f6-g7?? and succumbed to 16 ♕xg7+! ♔xg7 17 ♘f5++ ♔g8 18 ♘h6# (1-0).

It's worth noting that 16 ♘f5?, which sometimes works in positions like this, fails here to 16...♗xb2! (but not of course 16...♗xh6? 17 ♘xh6# or 16...gxf5 17 ♕xg7#).

MA09
Belsitzman – Rubinstein
Warsaw 1917

In this famous example, Black combined a light-square assault with an attack down the h-file and completed matters with 16...♕xh2+!, when White resigned in view of 17 ♔xh2 hxg3++ 18 ♔g1 ♖h1#.

(The preceding moves were 1 e4 e5 2 ♘f3 ♘c6 3 ♘c3 ♘f6 4 ♗b5 ♘d4 5 ♗c4 ♗c5 6 ♘xe5 ♕e7 7 ♘d3 d5 8 ♘xd5 ♕xe4+ 9 ♘e3 ♗d6 10 0-0 b5 11 ♗b3 ♗b7 12 ♘e1 ♕h4 13 g3 ♕h3 14 c3 h5 15 cxd4 h4 16 ♕e2? – it seems that 16 ♘f3 defends.)

MA10
Lahaye – Gommers
Hengelo (Under-16) 1996

This is another example of an attack at the intersection of the long diagonal and the h-file. If 30 ♕h7+ ♔f8

31 ♕xg7+ ♔e8, the black king can run, but 30 ♕h8+! forces immediate mate after 30...♗xh8 31 ♖xh8#.

MA11
Botvinnik – Keres
World Ch, Moscow/The Hague 1948

In dark-square attacks, the target is often g7 where, if it works, a knight sacrifice may be utterly deadly. In this case though, White sacrificed his rook: 21 ♖xg7+! ♔xg7 22 ♘h5+ ♔g6 (22...♔g8 23 ♘xf6+ is utterly hopeless for Black) 23 ♕e3! 1-0.

MA12
Hennings – Csulits
East German Ch, Annaberg-Buchholz 1965

Here White is again attacking on the dark squares and would dearly love to rip open the enemy king's carapace with 13 ♘xg7! *(D)*.

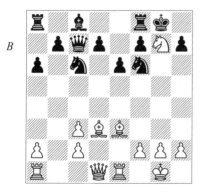

This is indeed correct though after 13...♔xg7 you needed to find the typical follow-up 14 ♗h6+ (since 14 ♕f3 is answered with 14...♘g8!, which is also very typical of such positions, defending the crucial dark squares) 14...♔xh6 (14...♔g8 is met by 15 ♕f3; or if 14...♔h8 then simply 15 ♗xf8) 15 ♕d2+ ♔h5 (15...♔g7 16 ♕g5+ ♔h8 17 ♕xf6+ ♔g8 and White has numerous wins, of which the cleanest of all is 18 ♕g5+ ♔h8 19 ♕h6) 16 ♖e3 ♘e5 17 ♖h3+ ♔g4 18 ♕e2+ ♔g5 19 ♕e3+ 1-0.

MA13
Wagman – Astengo
Genoa 1986

In a dark-square attack, a pawn on f6 can be incredibly powerful in combination with the queen. Here Black has managed to defend g7 for the moment but there is also a threat against h7.

It finished 18 ♕h6 ♘e6 19 ♖f4 ♖g8 20 ♕xh7+! and Black resigned in view of 20...♔xh7 21 ♖h4#.

Once this attack has been set up, then with the rook defending g7 there is usually only one defence – unless Black can counterattack – which is to play ...g5 (obviously not possible here) so as to make room for the king on g6.

MA14
Volzhin – Tunik
Russian Ch, Samara 2000

Here the pawn isn't yet on f6 but the pattern with the pawn on e5 and knight, typically on e4 and in any case ready to go to f6, always suggests ♘f6+ as a possibility.

In this case it was completely clear: after 19 ♘f6+! gxf6 (or 19...♗xf6 20 exf6 gxf6 21 ♕h6) 20 ♖e3 Black has no defence and he resigned at once.

MA15
Grekso – Nyers
Slovakian Under-18 Ch,
Komarno 1999

Obviously the same pattern also applies to Black. Here he has far too many attacking units in the vicinity of White's king and after 19...♘f3+ 20 ♗xf3 exf3 21 g3 White resigned, not waiting for 21...♖xh2! 22 ♔xh2 ♕h6+ 23 ♔g1 ♕h3.

MA16
Perifanis – Tsomis
Kallithea 1978

We move across now to the light-square attack against h7, starting with this very simple but also quite typical example of a combination to get the queen into the attack with tempo.

After 21 ♖h8+! Black resigned in view of 21...♔xh8 22 ♕h2+ ♔g8 23 ♕h7#.

MA17
Scholz – Matriciani
Hassloch 1996

This example is essentially the same, except that White now has to get rid of both rooks to activate the queen: 23 ♖h8+ ♔xh8 and Black resigned without waiting for 24 ♖h3+ ♔g8 25 ♖h8+! ♔xh8 26 ♕h3+ ♔g8 27 ♕h7+ ♔f8 28 ♕h8#.

MA18
Yates – Marin y Llovet
Hamburg Olympiad 1930

In this example, which I've chosen because of its absolutely forced nature, the target is again h7 but this time White gets at it through the 'Greek Gift' sacrifice: 11 ♗xh7+! and Black resigned at once in view of 11...♔xh7 12 ♕h5+ ♔g8 13 ♘g5 ♖d8 14 ♕h7+ ♔f8 15 ♕h8#.

MA19
Luthi – Leist
Zurich 1986

After 12 ♗xh7+ ♔xh7 13 ♘g5+ *(D)*:

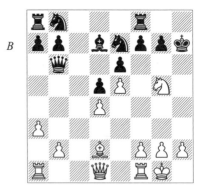

a) If 13...♔g8 14 ♕h5 ♖e8 15 ♕xf7+ ♔h8, 16 ♗b4! is possible because of the a3-pawn, threatening ♕h5+, ♕h7+ and ♕h8# and thus completely demolishing this as even a plausible defence. However, were the pawn on a2 then 16 ♖ae1 would still be decisive; e.g., if 16...♘f5, then 17 ♖e3 ♘xe3 18 fxe3, etc.

b) The knight on b8 blocks the back rank so that the rook isn't defended either on f8, or in one line h8. In the game Black tried 13...♔g6 but 14 ♕g4 (which is also the way White meets 13...♔h6) 14...f5 (if 14...f6, 15 ♘xe6+ ♔f7 16 ♕xg7+ ♔xe6 17 ♕xf8 wins easily) 15 ♕h4 was completely decisive because with the knight on b8 Black can't play 15...♖h8. The game ended quickly 15...f4 16 ♕h7+ ♔xg5 17 h4+ ♔g4 18 f3+ ♔g3 19 ♗e1# (1-0).

MA20
Pappier – Devcić
Buenos Aires 1981
Here the point of attack has moved across to f7 and in this case it's totally clear: 13 ♗xf7+! ♔xf7 14 ♕c4+ and then if 14...♔f8, 15 ♘g6#. Black tried 14...♘d5 but resigned after 15 ♘xd5 ♘b6 16 ♘xb6+ ♗e6 17 ♘xa8 ♖xa8 18 ♕e2 ♗xh4 19 ♕h5+.

MA21
de la Paz – Wohl
Havana 2001
Here the catastrophe occurred even earlier. The game had started 1 e4 e5 2 ♘f3 d6 3 ♗c4 ♗e7 4 c3 ♘f6 5 d3 0-0 6 ♗b3 ♘bd7 7 0-0 ♖e8?? and after 8 ♗xf7+ Black resigned immediately in view of 8...♔xf7 9 ♘g5+ ♔any 10 ♘e6 winning the queen.

MA22
Alekhine – Feldt
Simultaneous, Odessa 1916

In this position from a simultaneous display, the attack is again against the light squares but this time a knight is sacrificed on f7 and there is a mini king-hunt: 15 ♘f7! ♔xf7 (or 15...♗xf3 16 ♕xe6) 16 ♕xe6+! ♔g6 (16...♔xe6 17 ♘g5#; 16...♔f8 17 ♘g5) 17 g4! ♗e4 18 ♘h4#.

MA23
In this example position the attack again takes place on light squares, this time leading to a 'smothered mate': 1 ♕d5+ (but not 1 ♕b3+? ♔h8 2 ♘f7+ ♖xf7!) 1...♔h8 2 ♘f7+ ♔g8 (here if 2...♖xf7, 3 ♕xa8+) 3 ♘h6++ ♔h8 4 ♕g8+! ♖xg8 5 ♘f7#.

MA24
Chojnacki – Burzynski
Poznan 2001
Here a smothered mate occurred in an actual game. Black had just blundered horribly with 10...♖f8-e8?? (10...♗d6! was best) positively inviting 11 ♘xf7! ♔xf7 (if 11...♗xf3, then 12 gxf3 ♔xf7 13 ♕xe6+ ♔f8 14 ♗c4 wins) 12 ♘g5+ (12 ♕xe6+ ♔f8 13 ♘g5 ♗d5 is less clear, though 14 ♘xh7+ ♘xh7 15 ♕xd5 should still be sufficient to win) 12...♔g8 13 ♕xe6+ ♔h8 14 ♘f7+ ♔g8 15 ♘h6++ ♔h8 16 ♕g8+ ♘xg8 17 ♘f7# (1-0).

MA25
Nayer – S. Ionov
St Petersburg 2004
We conclude with some examples of sacrifices to rip open files to the castled

king, starting with this simple one from a Russian Championship semi-final.

24 ♖xg7+! caused instant resignation in view of 24...♚xg7 25 ♕g5+ ♚h8 26 ♕f6+ ♚g8 27 ♖g1# or 24...♚h8 25 ♖xh7+ ♚xh7 26 ♗f5+, mating.

MA26
Lovrić – Sinanović
Croatia Cup, Pula 1998

White's attacking lines intersect at g7 – and indeed I could also have included the example earlier as a dark-square attack.

18 ♘d7! cleared the decks and after 18...♕xd7, 19 ♖xg7+! ♚h8 (or 19...♚xg7 20 ♕g4+) 20 ♗xf6 ♘e8 21 ♖g8++! was the thematic way to conclude, forcing resignation in view of 21...♚xg8 22 ♕g4+ though 21 ♖xh7+ does also force mate.

MA27
Steinitz – Chigorin
World Ch (4), Havana 1892

24 ♖xh7+! ♚xh7 25 ♕h1+ ♚g7 26 ♗h6+ (26 ♕h6+ ♚f6 27 ♕h4+ ♚g7 28 ♗h6+ ♚h8 29 ♗xf8# also mates) 26...♚f6 27 ♕h4+ ♚e5 28 ♕xd4+ and Black resigned, not waiting for 28...♚f5 29 g4#.

MA28
Short – Ye Jiangchuan
Taiyuan 2004

Black, who was lost in any case, had just tried 26...♘f6x♘d5. After 27 ♕xh7+! he resigned immediately in

view of 27...♚xh7 28 ♖h3+ ♚g7 29 ♗h6+ ♚h8 30 ♗f8+ ♗h4 31 ♖xh4#.

MA29
J. Polgar – Karpov
Hoogeveen 2003

With so many white units ready to attack the king, it's unsurprising that White can strike and indeed a classic double bishop sacrifice is completely murderous.

After 25 ♗xh7+! ♚xh7 26 ♕h5+ Karpov resigned immediately without waiting for the sacrifice of the second bishop 26...♚g8 27 ♗xg7!, which is completely clear here because the rook is already on the third rank, viz.:

a) 27...♚xg7 28 ♖g3+.

b) 27...f5 28 ♕g6.

c) 27...f6 and then one way to win is 28 ♗xf8 (28 ♗xf6!? forces a speedy mate) 28...♖xe3 (28...♚xf8 29 ♖xe8+ or 28...♖xf8 29 ♖g3+) 29 ♕g6+ ♚xf8 30 ♕xf6+ followed by 31 ♖xe3.

MA30
S. Pedersen – Zygouris
World Under-16 Ch, Singapore 1990

This pattern, which is known as Boden's Mate, normally only applies to queenside castling and most often it is White who gets to play it. (Although in the original game, Schulder-Boden, London 1860, it was Black who mated by ...♕xc3+.)

After 19...0-0-0?? 20 ♕xc6+ Black resigned in view of immediate mate after 20...bxc6 21 ♗a6#.

The Back Rank

BR01
Szabo – Apsenieks
Kemeri 1939

In a lost position, Black had just tried 30...♕a6xb6, snapping off the enemy passed pawn. However, this meant that the queen no longer defended the a8-rook. Black needs two major pieces to guard a8 and so Szabo was able to finish off nicely with 31 ♕xa8! *(D)*.

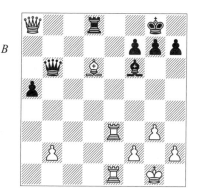

The end was 31...♕xd6 (31...♖xa8 is also met by 32 ♖e8+) 32 ♖e8+! 1-0.

BR02
O. Bernstein – Capablanca
Moscow 1914

In this famous example White has just optimistically captured a pawn on c3. After 28...♖xc3 29 ♖xc3 he'd obviously foreseen 29...♕b1+? 30 ♕f1 ♖d1?? 31 ♖c8+.

But Capablanca had seen deeper and after the vicious 29...♕b2! Bernstein resigned immediately in view of 30 ♕xb2 ♖d1# or 30 ♕e1 ♕xc3! 31 ♕xc3 ♖d1+.

BR03
Tuk – Assanova
Lublin 1969

The latter. White had seen that after 1...♖xc7 2 ♖xb4, 2...axb4?? fails to 3 ♖xa8+, but missed that instead 2...♖ac8 wins a rook owing to the threat of 3...♖c1+.

BR04
Unknown players
Yugoslavia 1949

No! After 1...♖c5!! *(D)* the tables were turned completely.

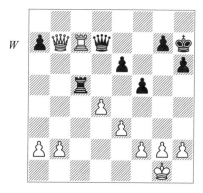

The best White can do is 2 ♖xc5 ♕xb7 so he resigned immediately.

BR05
Bruzon – Jobava
Havana 2005

18 ♗c5! brought the bishop into the attack since if 18...♕xc5, then 19

♕d8+!. Black tried 18...♖e8 but resigned immediately after 19 ♖d5.

BR06
Xie Jun – Seirawan
Jinan 2002
After 23 ♘f6+?? ♗xf6 24 ♗xf6 ♕e4! White resigned at once though she could have struggled on with 25 h3 ♕xg4 26 ♖xd8 threatening 27 ♗e7.

BR07
Damsky – Nezhmetdinov
Moscow 1966
25...♖e8! won on the spot since if 26 ♕xf6, then 26...♕xc1+! 27 ♘xc1 ♖e1#.

BR08
Douven – Greenfeld
Groningen 1988
The deflection 26 ♖c8! *(D)* exposed Black's back-rank weakness.

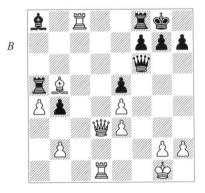

Of course if 26...♖xc8, then 27 ♕d8+!. Black tried 26...♕b6 but after 27 ♕d8! anyway had to resign.

BR09
Tisdall – J. Polgar
Reykjavik 1988
After 32...♖1h3! the only move to avoid instant material loss was 33 ♕e2 but then the unexpected 33...♕a4+! forced immediate resignation in view of 34 ♖xa4 ♖xa4+ 35 ♔b1 ♖h1+.

BR10
Alekhine – Frieman
Simultaneous, New York 1924
22 ♗xf6! *(D)* was decisive.

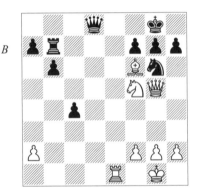

If 22...gxf6, then 23 ♕h6 ♕f8 24 ♖e8!, while 22...♕xf6 is met by 23 ♖e8+ ♘f8 24 ♘h6+! ♕xh6 25 ♖xf8+ ♔xf8 26 ♕d8#.

BR11
Mikenas – Bronstein
USSR Ch, Tallinn 1965
If 24...♕e1+, 25 ♕f1 defends. However, the geometry of the position allowed a quite beautiful finishing blow: 24...♖xa3!! and White resigned in view of 25 ♖xa3 ♕e1+, 25 ♕xa3 ♕e1+ 26

♖xe1 ♖xe1# or 25 bxa3 ♕xa1+ 26 ♖b1 ♖e1+!.

BR12

Marić – Gligorić
Belgrade 1962

After 19 ♗b7 ♖xc3 20 ♖xf5 the very beautiful 20...♖b3!, a precursor to Bronstein's combination above, won on the spot.

Stalemate

ST01

This is in some sense the fundamental position of endgame theory. It is, of course, very simple but you still have to get it right since a mistake instantly costs half a point.

Black plays 1...♔f8 and draws after 2 ♔e6 (or 2 ♔g6 ♔g8) 2...♔e8 3 f7+ ♔f8 4 ♔f6 stalemate.

If 1...♔e8?, then 2 ♔e6 ♔f8 3 f7 while 1...♔g8? 2 ♔g6 is slightly more interesting since 2...♔h8 invites 3 f7?? with another stalemate though 3 ♔f7 is easy.

ST02

Grabarczyk – Maciejewski
Polish Ch, Czestochowa 1993

We move swiftly on to something a bit more interesting. Here White should have noticed that the black king only has one escape-square on g7. After 1 ♔e3? (1 ♗d1 should win in the end though there's still hard work to be done) 1...♖g1! they agreed a draw immediately since 2 ♖xg1 is indeed

stalemate and 2 ♖h2 ♖g2! 3 ♖h3 ♖g3+! doesn't change matters materially.

ST03

The obvious 1 ♕xd5+ ♔xd5 2 ♔e2 loses after 2...♔c4 3 ♔d2 ♔b3 4 ♔c1 ♔a2 since the white king can't reach the corner but White can gain a tempo with 1 ♔e1! *(D)*.

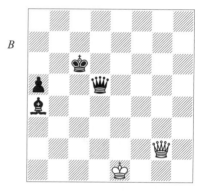

Now 1...♕xg2 is immediate stalemate and otherwise the white king is in time; for example, 1...♔c5 2 ♕xd5+ ♔xd5 3 ♔d2 ♔c4 4 ♔c1 and 5 ♔b1, etc.

ST04

Haznedaroglu – Malakhov
FIDE Knockout, Tripoli 2004

With his king pinned on the back rank and the black king looking relatively well covered, White looks in serious trouble but he drew in just two more moves with 107 ♕d8+ ♔e3 (otherwise the king can't escape the checks) 108 ♕d2+! ♖xd2 stalemate.

ST05
Pilnick – Reshevsky
USA Ch, New York 1942

Reshevsky had just blundered with 92...g4?, intending 93 ♕xg4 ♕e1+ and 94...♕g3+ to end matters. However, after 93 ♕f2! he had to agree an immediate draw in view of 93...♕xf2 stalemate – a pattern which occurs explicitly or implicitly quite often in queen endgames.

ST06
Klümper – Sölter
Bottrop 1971

The black king could have escaped the checks after 58...♔c2! 59 ♕e2+ ♔c3 60 ♕e1+ ♔c4.

However, he made the mistake of taking the last white pawn: 58...♔xa2? 59 ♕f2+ ♔b1 60 ♕e1+ ♔c2 61 ♕f2+ ♔d1 62 ♕f1+ ♔d2 63 ♕f2+ ♔c3 (he has to try to cross the third rank eventually) 64 ♕g3+! ♕xg3 stalemate.

ST07
Goldstein – Shakhnovich
Moscow 1946

White played 1 ♔e5? and after 1...gxf3 2 ♗xf3 (if 2 c7+ ♔c8 3 ♗xf3 {3 ♗f5+ ♖d7 draws – but would win with the king on e3}, 3...♖c1! 4 ♔d6 ♖c6+! forces a different stalemate) 2...♖d7!! 3 ♗d5 ♖b7! the draw was agreed.

ST08
Kotov – Pachman (variation)
Venice 1950

1...♔f5? loses to 2 ♖f7+ ♔e6 3 ♖f6+, but Black can save himself with 1...♖c6! 2 ♖xg6+ (if 2 ♔g4, then 2...♔d5 3 f5 ♖c4+; or 2 ♔e4 ♖c4+ 3 ♔e3 ♔f5 4 ♖f7+ ♔g4) 2...♔f5 3 ♖xc6 stalemate (or 3 ♖g8 ♖c3+).

ST09
Speelman – NN
Simultaneous, Ostend 2006

If 1 ♔xg5, then 1...♖xh3 2 f6+ ♔g8 3 ♖a8+ ♔h7 4 ♖f8 ♖h5+ 5 ♔f4 ♖a5 6 g5 ♖xg5! 7 ♖xf7+ ♔g8 draws. Therefore White has to arrange that Black keeps a pawn, which he does with 1 h4! gxh4 2 f6+ ♔h7 3 ♖a7 (D).

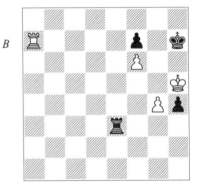

The conclusion was 3...♔g8 4 ♖a8+ ♔h7 5 ♖f8 h3 6 ♖xf7+ ♔g8 7 ♖g7+ ♔f8 8 ♖h7 h2 9 ♔g6 1-0.

ST10
Katišonok – Markhaus
USSR 1976

The white pawns are about to land but Black is able to use his own to force a draw:

1...♗d3+ 2 ♔xd3 a2+ 3 ♔b2 (or 3 ♔a1 b2+) 3...a1♕+ 4 ♔xa1 b2+ 5 ♔a2 b1♕+ 6 ♔xb1 (or 6 ♗xb1) stalemate.

ST11
G. Nadareishvili
Shakhmaty v SSSR, 1961

In this study, White has to avoid stalemating Black. If 1 ♔b6, then 1...g5! 2 ♖xg5 ♔h2 3 ♔c5 h3 4 ♔d4 ♔h1 5 ♔e3 h2 draws but he can gain time by blockading the g-pawn: 1 ♖g5! ♔h2 2 ♔b6 h3 3 ♔c5 ♔h1 4 ♔d4 h2 5 ♔e3 g6 6 ♖g3! g5 7 ♔f2 g4 8 ♖a3 g3+ 9 ♔xg3 ♔g1 10 ♖a1#.

ST12
P. Keres
The Chess World, 1933

In this simple but quite elegant study by the great Paul Keres, White forces stalemate by deflecting the enemy bishop as it rushes to prevent the b-pawn from promoting: 1 ♕xc3! ♗f3+ 2 ♕xf3 exf3 3 b5 ♗xf2 4 b6 ♗xd4 5 b7 ♗e5 6 b8♕+ ♗xb8 stalemate.

Pawn Promotion

PP01
a) If White is to move, he wins with 1 b6! cxb6 (or 1...axb6 2 c6 bxc6 3 a6) 2 a6 bxa6 3 c6 and the c-pawn strides on.

b) If it is Black's turn to play, he can defend only by 1...b6! (not 1...a6? 2 c6; nor 1...c6? 2 a6) 2 axb6 axb6 3 cxb6 cxb6 with a draw (Black can

capture on b5 but White arranges to meet this with ♔b3, taking the opposition).

PP02
Knights tend to be ineffective at the edge of the board and are particularly weak in combat with passed rook's pawns.

Here 1 ♘b7+ ♘xb7 2 a6 wins because after 2...♔c7/c8 White ignores the knight and plays 3 a7!.

PP03
Shirov – Atalik
Sarajevo 2004

Here another deflection finishes things. 39 ♖ad2 ♖c6 40 ♕e8+ ♕xe8 41 dxe8♕+ ♔xe8 42 ♖d8+ ♔f7 43 ♖2d7+ should win but Shirov was much more incisive: 39 ♖e6+! ♔xd7 (or 39...♔xe6 40 ♕e8+) 40 ♖d2+ and Atalik resigned.

PP04
V. Belov – Lautier
Moscow 2004

It looks as though the c-pawn is about to be surrounded but Lautier showed otherwise with the splendid 31...♗e2+!! (not 31...♗c6? 32 ♖c1) 32 ♔g3 ♗d1 33 ♗xc2 ♗xc2 and White resigned on move 49.

PP05
Blackburne – Winawer
Berlin 1891

Of course White is winning easily but he does have to take a modicum of care since immediate promotion would release too much energy.

If 38 b8♕??, then 38...♕c1+! 39 ♔h2 ♕f4+ forces stalemate or perpetual check.

However, after the simple 38 ♗xg6+ Black resigned.

PP06
Potkin – Izoria
Dos Hermanas
(Internet knockout) 2003

White pursues the enemy knight to the fatal square c4 and then wins it due to the power of the f-pawn: 56 ♔c3 ♘b1+ 57 ♔b2! ♘d2 58 ♔c2 ♘c4 59 ♗d5+! ♔xf6 (or 59...♔xd5 60 f7) 60 ♗xc4 ♔e5 61 ♔d2 and in this hopeless position Black lost on time.

PP07
Khalifman – Campora
Dos Hermanas 2003

Here White is able to make a breakthrough to free the g6-pawn.

42 ♗xf6! gxf6 43 ♖e8+ and Black resigned in view of 43...♕xe8 44 g7+ ♔xg7 (or 44...♔f7 45 ♕xe8+ ♔xe8 46 g8♕+) 45 ♕xe8, when his pieces are hopelessly tied up.

PP08
Kröncke – Levin
Hamburg 2003

The attack on g7 looks dangerous but the massive passed pawn on e3 proved to be the decisive factor: 27...♗d4! (such is the power of the e-pawn that even 27...♕d1+ is quite good, though

after 28 ♕xd1 e2 29 ♕e1 ♗f2 30 ♕xf2 e1♕+ 31 ♕g1 ♕d2 32 ♘e5 ♕xc2 33 ♗d4 ♕xa2 White can still fight) 28 ♗xd4 ♕xd4 29 ♕xd4 e2 30 ♘f6+ gxf6 31 ♕g4+ ♔h8 and White resigned.

PP09
Grishchuk – Leko
Moscow (rapid) 2002

Leko played 41...♕xd2 and later only drew.

Instead 41...♖xd3 42 ♖xd3 ♖xd3 43 ♕xc3 ♖xd1+ wins on the spot. 44 ♕c1 can be met by either 44...bxa2+ or 44...♖xc1+ 45 ♔xc1 bxa2.

PP10
Bezgodov – Bachin
Russian Ch, Krasnoiarsk 2003

The simple but effective 33 ♕xc6! caused instant resignation.

PP11
Topalov – Bareev
Wijk aan Zee 2004

Bareev unpinned his g2-rook with 47...♔f8 (47...♔h7 or indeed 47...♔h8 would also have been sufficient but of course it makes sense to go towards the enemy passed pawn). The game concluded 48 ♖xg2 (48 ♖a1 is met by 48...♖b7; or 48 ♖f1 ♖b2 49 d5 ♖b1 50 ♔g1 f2+ 51 ♔g2 ♖g7+ 52 ♔xf2 ♖f7+) 48...f2!! – the point. If 49 ♖xf2 ♖xf2 the white king remains confined to the back rank and so ...♖b2-b1+ follows. Topalov therefore tried 49 ♖g1 but resigned after 49...f1♕!.

PP12
Malakhov – Zviagintsev
Poikovsky 2004

After 38...♕h4+ 39 ♔g1 ♕h2+ 40 ♔f1 ♕h1+ 41 ♔g1 e3! 42 ♕xh1 e2+ 43 ♔g1 d2! White resigned in the face of the avalanche.

PP13
Ermenkov – Sax
Warsaw 1969

If 44...d2, then 45 ♕a1+! followed by 46 d8♕ wins, so Black continued 44...♕xf1+ 45 ♔xf1 d2 46 ♕xf3 ♖c1+, which was apparently very strong until White hit him with the superb 47 ♕d1!! *(D)*.

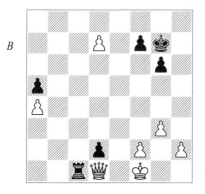

This caused instant resignation in view of 47...♖xd1+ 48 ♔e2 ♖b1 (or 48...♖e1+ 49 ♔xd2 and the pawn can't be stopped) 49 d8♕ d1♕+ 50 ♕xd1 ♖xd1 51 ♔xd1, when with an extra pawn White is winning easily.

We conclude with a couple of examples of underpromotion, which is usually to a knight since it can give check but occasionally to a rook or bishop to avoid giving stalemate.

PP14
Labone – NN
1889

This pattern occurs in a number of studies and (possibly apocryphal) games such as this. 1 ♖f8+ ♖xf8 2 ♕xh7+! ♔xh7 3 gxf8♘+! wins.

PP15
T. Gorgiev
Tidskrift för Schack, 1959

In this study, White's task is to force the same pattern as in the previous example. He does so by playing 1 e7 ♕xe7 2 b7+ ♔d7 3 c8♕+ ♖xc8 4 ♕d4+ ♔c7 5 ♕b6+ ♔b8 (if 5...♔xb6 6 bxc8♘+ ♔c5 7 ♘xe7 a5 8 ♔e4 a4 9 ♘d5 a3 10 ♘c3 ♔c4 11 ♘a2 ♔b3 12 e6 ♔xa2 13 e7 ♔b1 14 e8♕ a2 White is just winning: 15 ♕b5+ ♔c2 16 ♕c4+ ♔b2 17 ♕b4+ ♔c2 18 ♕a3 ♔b1 19 ♕b3+ ♔a1 20 ♕c3+ ♔b1 21 ♔d3 a1♕ 22 ♕c2#) 6 ♕a7+! ♔xa7 7 bxc8♘+!.

Finger Exercises

FE01
Gelfand – Lutz
Dortmund 2002

34 ♖d1 is completely obvious but Black seems to have a defence in 34...c5 35 bxc5 ♘xc5 36 ♖xd4 ♘b3, forking rook and bishop. Then, however, comes the sting in the tail: 37

♖e4! and Black resigned in view of 37...♘xa5 38 ♖e8#.

FE02
Donaldson Akhmylovskaya – Wang Pin
China – USA, Shanghai 2002

Black played 41...♖d1+ 42 ♔h2 and now not 42...♘g4+?? 43 ♗xg4 ♕xg4 44 ♖xh6+ but 42...♕xg2+! and White resigned in view of 43 ♗xg2 ♘g4#.

FE03
Spassky – Korchnoi
Candidates match (7), Kiev 1968

After 35 ♕h6+! Black resigned due to 35...♔xh6 36 ♖h1# or 35...♔g8 36 ♖c8+ ♖f8 37 ♖xf8#.

FE04
Eingorn – Van Wely
European Clubs Cup, Kallithea 2002

After 24...♗c5?, 25 ♕f3! (D) won on the spot.

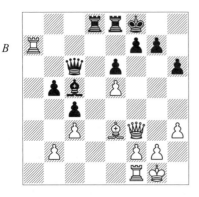

25...♕xf3 is met by the *zwischenzug* 26 ♗xc5+.

FE05
Hort – Radulski
Hoogeveen 2002

Such is the tension here that there is really only one move to consider: 39 ♕xf7+!. Depending on the exact position this could win, draw by perpetual, or indeed lose, but in this case White wins: 39...♔xf7 (if 39...♔h6, then 40 ♔xh1 ♕xg3 41 ♖a2, etc.) 40 ♖bxb7+ ♔f6 41 ♖f7#.

FE06
Salman – Molander
Curaçao 2002

The one move White mustn't play is 37 ♖xc7??. He did so and after the discovered attack 37...♘xd5! 38 ♖xf7 and the intermediate checks 38...♘xe3+ 39 ♔f2 ♘xg4+ 40 ♔g3 Black calmly recaptured 40...♖xf7 with a dead won game.

FE07
Hebden – Laubsch
Hastings Challengers 2002/3

After 27...♗c2?, 28 ♗xf7+! won a vital pawn: 28...♔xf7 (28...♕xf7 29 ♖xc2 ♖ad8 looks a bit better – but not 29...♖xa2? 30 ♖c7 with a winning attack) 29 ♕c7+ ♗e7 30 ♖xc2 and White had a huge advantage. In fact he won in just four more moves: 30...♖ac8 31 ♕f4+ ♔g8 32 ♖xc8 ♖xc8 33 ♕e5 ♖d8? 34 ♕xe7 1-0.

FE08
Timman – Topalov
Wijk aan Zee 2003

53...♕c4!! was decisive (but not 53...g2? 54 ♖c8+ ♕xc8 55 ♕xc8+ ♔e7 {55...♔f7 56 ♕f5+; 55...♔g7 56 ♕g4+} 56 ♕c5+ and White wins): 54 ♕a8+ (54 ♖xc4 f1♕+ 55 ♔a2 ♕xc4+) 54...♔e7 55 ♕xa7+ ♗c7 and White resigned.

FE09
Lugovoi – Lastin

38 ♗h6! forced instant resignation. Obviously if 38...♔xh6, then 39 ♕h8# but it's also vital that after 38...♗xf2+ 39 ♖xf2 ♖c1+ White has the backward move 40 ♗xc1!. Since the bishop's role is to support the queen on g7, it would be possible in a game, calculating in advance, to miss this very simple riposte.

FE10
Tiviakov – Ahmed
Dhaka 2003

30 ♘xg6!! crashed through at an apparent strong point in the opponent's defences. Black resigned in view of 30...♘xg6 (or 30...fxg6 31 f7+ ♔g7 32 ♕h6#) 31 ♕xh7+ ♔f8 32 ♕xh8+! ♘xh8 33 ♖xh8#.

FE11
Ibragimov – Roiz
Dos Hermanas
(Internet knockout) 2003

After the deflection 37 ♗a5! Black resigned due to 37...♕xa5 (37...♕xb7 38 cxb7 and Black cannot prevent the promotion of the b-pawn) 38 ♕f7+ ♔h8 39 ♕f8#.

FE12
Shamkovich – Kremenetsky
Moscow 1963

22 ♖xh7+! *(D)* caused instant resignation.

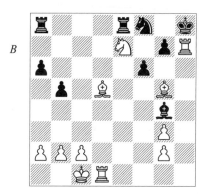

Mate is forced after either 22...♔xh7 23 ♖h1+ or 22...♘xh7 23 ♘g6#. Very simple, but it's still necessary to see it.

FE13
Ernst – Timoshenko
Tallinn 1989

After 29...♕xf2+! 30 ♖xf2 ♖d1+ White resigned.

FE14
Mariani – Zichichi
Italian Ch, Sottomarina 1970

After 19...♘g3+! White's best is to play 20 ♔g1 though he loses a whole exchange. Instead he played 20 hxg3 hxg3+ 21 ♔g1 ♘c4 (21...♘xd3 is also quite enough) and White resigned in view of the familiar pattern 22 ♗xc4 ♖h1+! 23 ♔xh1 ♕h5+ 24 ♔g1 ♕h2#.

FE15
Elbilia – Shirov
France 1993

The pin seems to give White some hope but Shirov unpinned with the venomous 22...♘e4!! *(D)*.

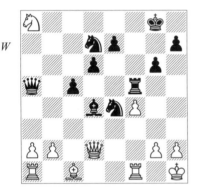

Now 23 ♕xa5 fails to 23...♘g3+ 24 hxg3 ♖h5# and 23 ♕e2 to 23...♕a6!. 23 ♕d1 is relatively best but after 23...♕xa8 Black is totally winning so White resigned on the spot.

FE16
M. Gurevich – Gelfand
Cap d'Agde 2002

29...♕xe6! (removing the guard from d1; 29...h5 30 ♕e2 ♕xe6 is equally effective) 30 ♕xe6 ♖d1+ 31 ♔h2 ♗g1+ and White resigned in view of 32 ♔h1 ♗f2+ 33 ♔h2 ♗g3#.

FE17
Hartvig – Edvardsen
Politiken Cup, Copenhagen 2003

37 ♕h5+! and Black resigned due to 37...♔xh5 38 ♖xh7#.

FE18
Hvenekilde – Skytte
Politiken Cup, Copenhagen 1999

After 61 ♔g6?? ♖f6+! White resigned because of 62 gxf6 ♕xf6+ 63 ♔h5 ♕h6# or 62 ♔h5 g6+ 63 ♔h6 ♕h4+ 64 ♗h5 ♕xh5#.

FE19
Hector – Gunnarsson
European Team Ch, Plovdiv 2003

After 40...♕xf4 41 ♖h8+! ♔xh8 42 ♖h5++ Black resigned in view of 42...♔g8 43 ♕h8+ ♔f7 44 ♖h7#.

FE20
Bologan – Palo
Skanderborg 2003

Rather amazingly, there's no defence to checkmate in just three more moves after 32 c3! ♗xa5 33 ♖b7! and 34 ♗a4# is unstoppable.

FE21
Tiviakov – Smirin
European Team Ch, Plovdiv 2003

a) If 23 ♖a7, then 23...♗d2+ (not 23...♕xb2 24 ♕xf8+) 24 ♕xd2 (24 ♔d1?? ♕b3+) 24...♕xc6. Black is certainly lost but can try to play on.

b) 23 ♖b6! ♕a8 24 ♕xf8+ and Black resigned since after 24...♕xf8 25 ♖b8 there's absolutely no chance.

FE22
Arlandi – Kurajica
European Team Ch, Plovdiv 2003

a) The unprotected queen on c3 opposite her counterpart is a serious tactical weakness, which calls for a discovery by the knight.

b) White had just played 26 ♔g1-g2??, which indeed prevents ...♘f3 from being with check. Nevertheless 26...♘f3! still caused resignation since after 27 ♕xf6 the *zwischenzug* 27...♘xe1+ wins the exchange and destroys the white position.

FE23
Shumiakina – Sebag
European Clubs Cup (women), Rethymnon 2003

57...h5+! 58 ♔xh5 ♕f5+ 59 ♔h6 ♕h7# was checkmate!

FE24
Levenfish – Riumin
Moscow 1936

In the game White backed off and after 27 ♘g3? later drew.

Instead the sacrifice 27 ♘f6+! gxf6 28 exf6 (D) screams out to be played.

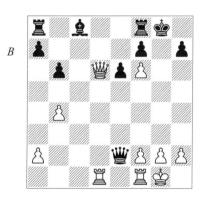

Perhaps White thought that 28...e5 was a defence, preventing 29 ♕g3+,

but then 29 ♕xf8+! ♔xf8 30 ♖d8# is mate.

FE25
Kudrin – Basque
Philadelphia 2003

20 ♘e3! drove the rook away and after 20...♖xb2 21 ♖c1 ♕b4 22 ♖c8+ ♔d7 23 ♖xg8 White had won a whole rook.

FE26
Souleidis – Espig
Bundesliga 2003/4

After 26...♗xd4 27 ♕xd4 ♖e1+ 28 ♗g1 ♖xg1+! 29 ♔xg1 ♘xf3+ White resigned.

FE27
Andersson – Dreev
Dordrecht (blitz) 2004

20 ♗xa6! (D) would have won an important pawn.

If 20...♖xa6, then 21 ♖xc6! bxc6 22 ♕b7+. Presumably, Black would have continued 20...♖b8 maintaining fair

chances in a blitz game – but much less good than with the a-pawn still intact.

FE28
Gild. Garcia – Zapata
Medellin 1992

19 ♘f6+! screams out to be played. The question is whether it works and indeed after 19...gxf6 20 ♖g5+ Black resigned in view of 20...♔h8 21 ♕h6 fxg5 22 ♕f6+ ♔g8 23 ♗e5.

FE29
Belavenets – Smyslov
Leningrad/Moscow 1939

Black's bishop is *en prise* but with the white king in trouble it didn't matter. After 35...♖dd2!! the main point was that if 36 ♖xe3, 36...g5! closes the net. White tried 36 ♖g1 (36 f4 ♗xf4+ 37 ♔h4 ♖h2 also finishes things off) and after 36...g5 he resigned.

FE30
Mason – S. Clarke
British League (4NCL) 2002/3

White powered through with 25 ♖xe4! dxe4 26 ♕f8+ ♖g8 27 ♘g6+ and Black resigned due to 27...hxg6 28 ♕h6#.

FE31
Vasiukov – Kholmov
USSR Spartakiad, Moscow 1964

After 25 ♘xc5 ♕xc5, 26 ♗xg7! forced instant resignation in view of 26...♗xg7 27 ♕h5 h6 28 ♗h7+ ♔xh7 29 ♕xc5.

FE32
Atalik – Kožul
Sarajevo 2004

35...♘xe4+ 36 fxe4 ♕h2+ 37 ♔e1 (or 37 ♔e3 ♗g5+) 37...♗h4+ would have won on the spot.

FE33
Kasimdzhanov – Almasi
FIDE Knockout, Tripoli 2004

Black seems to be doing well here because if 33 ♕d7+ ♔h6 the checks end. But White had foreseen a beautiful way to emerge with a decisive advantage: 33 ♕xf6+! ♕xf6 34 ♖d7+ ♔h6 35 ♖xf6 and Black resigned.

FE34
T.L. Petrosian – Drozdovsky
World Junior Ch, Kochin 2004

The pressure proved immediately decisive after 33 ♗b6! ♗c7 (33...♖d6? 34 ♗xd8) 34 ♗xc7 ♕xc7 35 ♕a8+! and Black resigned in view of the line 35...♖d8 36 ♖e8+! ♖xe8 37 ♕xe8#.

FE35
Terzić – Nurkić
Bosnia 1994

The solution is just a single move but a very pretty one – and one which you could certainly miss on a bad day. After 17 ♕xe5+!! Black resigned in view of mate next move – 17...dxe5 18 ♗c5# or 17...fxe5 18 ♗g5#.

FE36
Haba – Lechtynsky
Czech Ch, Karlovy Vary 2005

After 29 ♖xf6! Black resigned at once in view of 29...♕xf6 30 ♖xb6! ♖xb6 (or 30...♕xb6 31 ♕xg7#) 31 ♕c8+.

FE37
Elianov – Wang Yue
Aeroflot Open, Moscow 2005
With several pieces defending his king, Black is a move away from survival but a simple forced sequence finished him off: 28 ♖xf5! exf5 29 ♖h8+! and Black resigned, not waiting for 29...♔xh8 30 ♕h5+ ♔g8 31 ♕h7#.

FE38
Tomashevsky – I. Popov
Russian Junior Ch, Noiabrsk 2005
Of course, 31 ♖xg6 is the move to look at and it caused instant resignation because of 31...♖xg6 32 ♗xf5 ♗xf5 33 ♕xf5 ♖ag8 34 ♕xh5+ ♖h6 35 ♕f7+ ♔h8 36 ♕xg8#.

FE39
Kotrotsos – Stiri
Iraklion 2005
After 12 ♕f8+!! Black resigned in view of 12...♖xf8 13 ♘d6+ ♔e7 14 ♘f5++ ♔e8 15 ♘xg7#. The opening moves of this miniature were 1 e4 c5 2 ♘f3 e6 3 b3 b6 4 d4 cxd4 5 ♘xd4 ♗b7 6 ♘b5 a6 7 ♘d6+ ♗xd6 8 ♕xd6 ♗xe4 9 ♗a3 ♘f6 10 ♘d2 ♘c6 11 ♘c4 b5?.

FE40
Dobrev – Boichev
Sunny Beach 2005

35 ♕g8+! ♔e7 (or 35...♔xg8 36 ♘g6+ ♔f7 37 ♖f8#) 36 ♘g6+ ♖xg6 37 ♕e8+ and Black resigned as it is mate next move.

FE41
E. Atalik – Skripchenko
Biel (Ladies) 2006
The interference 28 ♖c6! cuts off the defence of d6 and after 28...♗xc6 29 ♕xd6+ ♔g7 30 ♗h6+ ♔g8 31 ♕g3+ Black resigned.

FE42
N. Popov – Novopashin
Beltsy 1979
This is a one-move problem – but what a move! 32 ♕h6+!! and Black resigned in view of 32...gxh6 (32...♔xh6 33 ♖h8#) 33 ♖xb7+, after which the rook cleans up along the seventh rank: 33...♗d7 34 ♖xd7+ ♘e7 35 ♖xe7+ ♕f7 36 ♖exf7#.

FE43
Moreno Carnero – Van Wely
Villarrobledo (rapid) 2006
After 27 ♕xh7+ Black resigned in view of the lines 27...♘xh7 28 ♘g6# and 27...♔xh7 28 ♖h3+ ♗h4 29 ♖xh4#. But note that the alternative sequence 27 ♘g6+? ♘xg6 28 ♕xh7+ doesn't work because after 28...♔xh7 29 ♖h3+ either 29...♗h4 or 29...♘h4 defends for Black.

FE44
Kr. Georgiev – A. Spasov
Sunny Beach 2005

A simple but effective knight-fork combination was fatal. After 21 ♗xe6 fxe6 22 ♖c7! Black resigned.

FE45

In this illustrative example, White's cross-pin wins the house after the pretty 1 ♖c7! ♗xc7 2 ♕e4! *(D)*.

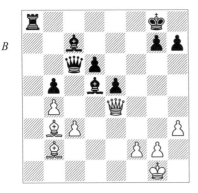

FE46

Smyslov – Oll
Rostov 1993

The ex-World Champion ignored the attack on his rook with 29 g4+! ♔xe4 (else 30 fxg5 next move) 30 ♘f2+ ♔xf4 31 ♖g1!, and there was no adequate defence against 32 ♗d2#.

FE47

Khalifman – Serper
St Petersburg 1994

White powered through in the obvious way with 28 ♖xb7+! ♔xb7 29 ♖xc7+! ♔xc7 30 ♕xa7+ ♔c8 and now the relatively quiet but deadly 31 d6 sealed matters.

FE48

Speelman – Peng Xiaomin
Erevan Olympiad 1996

I still thought I was fighting until my opponent hit me with the beautiful 44...♖xg3+!! 45 ♔xg3 ♗h4+! *(D)*.

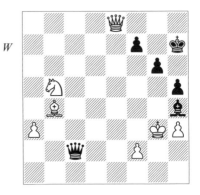

46 ♔xh4 (or 46 ♔h2 ♕xf2+ 47 ♔h1 ♕f3+ 48 ♔g1 ♗f2+ 49 ♔f1 ♗g3+ 50 ♔g1 ♕f2+ 51 ♔h1 ♕h2#) 46...♕xf2+ 47 ♔g5 ♕f5+ 48 ♔h4 ♕f4# (0-1).

Mixed Bag

MB01

Ivanchuk – Topalov
Monaco (Amber blindfold) 2004

48 ♖f8! forced instant resignation since after 48...♖xg7, 49 ♖f2# is a snap checkmate.

MB02

P.H. Nielsen – Golubev
ACP Internet blitz 2004

26 ♘g6+! smashed open the black king's fortress and after 26...hxg6 27

♕h4+ Black resigned due to 27...♔g8 28 ♗d5+ ♖f7 29 ♕xd8+.

MB03
I. Sokolov – P.H. Nielsen
Swedish Team Ch 2003/4
22...♖8a7?? fatally weakened the back rank and after 23 ♖c8+! Black had to resign at once.

MB04
J. Åkesson – K. Ong
Swedish Ch, Gothenburg 2004
The thematic 23...♕h4! exploited White's light-square weaknesses (but not 23...♖xh2? 24 ♖xe4). After 24 ♗h5 (24 gxh4 ♖g6+) 24...♕xh2+! 25 ♔xh2 ♖xh5+ White resigned.

MB05
Akimov – Pridorozhny
St Petersburg 2000
You should always be alert to the possibility of the opponent castling, and here 12 ♕xd8+! caused instant resignation in view of 12...♔xd8 13 0-0-0+! ♕d5 14 ♘xd5, when White is a whole rook up.

The preceding moves in this miniature were 1 e4 c5 2 c3 d5 3 exd5 ♕xd5 4 d4 ♘c6 5 ♘f3 e5 6 ♗b5 cxd4 7 ♗xc6+ bxc6 8 cxd4 ♗a6 9 ♘c3 ♗b4 10 dxe5 ♕e4+ 11 ♗e3 ♖d8??.

MB06
Rossolimo – Romanenko
Salzburg 1948
13 ♖e8+! *(D)* included the queen in the attack with tempo.

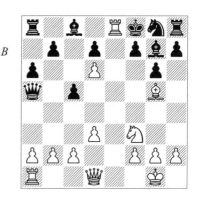

After 13...♔xe8 14 ♕e2+ ♔f8 15 ♗e7+ ♔e8 (15...♘xe7 16 ♕xe7+ ♔g8 17 ♘g5) 16 ♗d8+! ♔xd8 17 ♘g5 Black resigned as 17...♘h6 18 ♕e7# is checkmate.

MB07
Alekhine – Reshevsky
Kemeri 1937
After 35 ♖xb8+! ♔xb8 36 ♕xe5+! Black resigned (36...fxe5 37 ♖f8+).

MB08
Coggan – Foster
Boston 1937
1 ♗xf6 ♗xf6 (or 1...gxf6 2 ♕h6 and mate soon follows) 2 ♕xh7+! ♔xh7 3 ♖h5+ ♔g8 4 ♘g6 and there's no defence against 5 ♖h8#.

MB09
Kupreichik – Tseshkovsky
USSR Ch, Moscow 1976
27 ♘c8+! cuts the back rank, winning on the spot in view of 27...♘c5 (obviously if 27...♔e8, then 28 ♕e7#) 28 ♕xc5+! ♕xc5 29 ♖d8#.

MB10
Kirton – Gentes
Winnipeg 2000

30 ♕xf8+! ♗xf8 31 ♘f7+! and Black resigned due to 31...♖xf7 32 ♖g8#.

MB11
Doggers – Henrichs
Hoogeveen 2005

Instead of 33...♕xd4?? most moves win; for example, 33...♗xg5 34 ♖g4 f6 is quite good enough.

However, after 33...♕xd4?? White played 34 ♕xh7+! ♔xh7 35 ♖h4+ ♔g6 (or 35...♔g8 36 ♖h8#) 36 ♖h6+ and Black resigned, not waiting for the very pretty 36...♔xg5 37 ♗f4#.

MB12
Speelman – Van Blitterswijk
Dutch League 2006/7

After 30 ♕xg6 ♕xf4 31 ♕xg7+! Black resigned.

MB13
Y. Vovk – Shishkin
Odessa 2006

After 22 ♕e3? ♕f1+! Black unpinned by force, ending up a whole piece ahead and so forcing instant resignation.

MB14
Vigo Allepuz – F. Cruz
Sitges 2006

The white rook is pinned against the queen and so 35...♖e2+! won on the spot.

MB15
Turner – A. Martin
London 1997

After 20 ♗f5 ♗xf5 21 ♕xf5 ♕h1+! White resigned in view of 22 ♔xh1 ♘g3++ 23 ♔g1 ♖h1#.

MB16
Beshukov – Dvoirys
Hoogeveen 2003

27...♘xh2! (27...♘e3 also seems to be good enough) crashed through: 28 ♗xh2 ♖xg2! 29 ♔xg2 ♖g8+ 30 ♗g3 (or: 30 ♔h1 ♕f3#; 30 ♔f1 ♕h3+) 30...♖xg3+ 31 ♕xg3 fxg3 and Black was winning easily. Indeed it ended 32 ♖d2 e4 33 ♖g1 ♘e5 0-1.

MB17
Sambuev – Smirnov
Russian Ch, Krasnoiarsk 2003

59 ♘g5! forces a way in. 59...hxg5 (or 59...♗xg3 60 ♘xe6 ♗xh4 61 ♘d4 ♔a8 62 e6 ♗f6 63 ♘xf5 h4 64 e7 ♗xe7 65 ♘xe7 h3 66 ♘f5) 60 hxg5 ♗c5 61 ♔d3 ♗e7 62 ♔e2 and the king strolls in by ♔f3-g2-h3-h4xh5, etc.

MB18
Zviagintsev – Kasimdzhanov
Essen 2002

Unfortunately 23...f6 fatally weakened the light squares and after 24 ♕g6! Black actually resigned on the spot, with full justification:

a) 24...fxe5 25 ♗e6+ ♔h8 26 fxe5 ♕a3 27 ♗f5 ♔g8 28 ♕h7+ ♔f8 (or 28...♔f7 29 ♗e6+ ♔xe6 30 ♕f5#) 29 ♗e6+ ♗f6 30 ♕g8+ ♔e7 31 ♕f7#.

b) 24...♗f8 25 ♗f5 is equally fatal after 25...fxe5 26 ♕h7+ ♔f7 27 fxe5 ♕a3, when the cleanest is 28 ♗e6++ ♔xe6 (if 28...♔e8, then 29 ♕g6+ ♔e7 30 ♕f7#; or 28...♔e7 29 ♖f7+ ♔e8 30 ♕g6) 29 ♕f5+ ♔e7 30 ♕f7#.

MB19
Speelman – Flear
British Ch, Torquay 2002

He (or rather I) had missed that after 17 ♗f4 dxe3 18 ♗xh6?? Black can play simply 18...♘e8!, winning a piece. The knight had gone from e8 to c7 only half a dozen moves earlier and since it was clearly *en route* to an active square like d5 I missed that it could go back. The moral is to look for all your opponent's possible moves, especially when you think he may have no defence.

MB20
Motylev – Timofeev
Russian Ch, Krasnoiarsk 2003

After 36 ♖f8+ (but not 36 ♕e8+? ♔h7 and Black wins) Black is lost because if 36...♔h7, then 37 g6+! ♔xg6 (37...♖xg6 38 ♕xd5) 38 ♕e8+ ♔h7 39 ♖h8#. Instead he tried 36...♕g8 but after 37 ♖xg8+ ♔xg8 38 ♕e8+ ♔h7 39 ♕xe4+ g6 40 ♕e5 the queen dominates the board and after 40...♖a6+ 41 ♔b1 hxg5 42 hxg5 ♖a7 43 ♕d4 ♖a8 44 ♕d7+ ♔h8 45 ♕b7 Black resigned.

MB21
Reiner – Steinitz
Vienna 1860

16...♕h4! 17 ♖g2 (of course if 17 ♖xh4, then 17...♖g1#) 17...♕xh2+ 18 ♖xh2 ♖g1#.

MB22
Keres – Szabo
Hungary – USSR, Budapest 1955

21 ♖xg7! ♔xg7 22 ♕f6+ ♔f8 (or 22...♔g8 23 ♕xh6 f5 24 exf6 ♖e7 25 fxe7) 23 ♗g6 and Black resigned in view of 23...♖e7 24 ♕h8#.

MB23
Grishchuk – Smirnov
Izmir 2004

45 ♗b3! ♘c4 (the best chance; if 45...♕xb3, then simply 46 ♗f6; or 45...♘d7 46 ♕h6+) 46 ♗xc4 ♕xc4 47 ♕h6+! (but not, of course, 47 ♗f6?? ♕c1+ 48 ♔h2 ♕f4+) 47...♔g8 48 ♗f6 and Black resigned.

MB24
Ehlvest – Neverov
Aeroflot Open, Moscow 2005

27 ♕g6! *(D)* forced liquidation to a completely winning endgame.

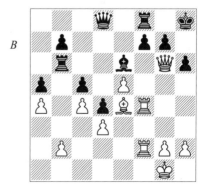

After 27...fxg6 28 ♖xf8+ ♕xf8 29 ♖xf8+ ♔h7, 30 ♗d5! tied down almost all of Black's pieces. After 30...h5 (or 30...g5 31 ♗e4+ g6 32 ♖f6) 31 h4 g5 32 ♗e4+ g6 33 ♖f6 gxh4 34 ♗xg6+ ♔g7 Black resigned, not waiting for 35 ♗f7.

MB25
Eriksson – Hellsten
Swedish Ch, Gothenburg 2006
a) The game ended 23 ♔b1? ♗e4+ 24 ♔a2 ♕xa3+! 25 bxa3 ♖c2+ 26 ♔b1 ♖d2+ 27 ♔a1 ♘b3# (0-1).

b) After 23 bxc3 (23 ♔d2 ♖g3 24 hxg3 ♗xh1 leaves Black a piece ahead) 28...♕xa3+ 24 ♔d2 ♘xc4+ 25 ♔e2 ♕b2+ 26 ♔f1 ♘d2+! 27 ♕xd2 ♕b5+ 28 ♕e2 (28 ♔g1 ♕xe5 is much worse) 28...♕xe2+ 29 ♔xe2 ♗xh1 30 ♖xh1 ♖xc3 Black has some advantage.

MB26
Tukmakov – Zhukova
Odessa/Istanbul (blitz) 2006
She could have forced immediate mate with 37...♘g3+ 38 ♔h2 ♘f1+! 39 ♔h1 ♕xh3+! 40 gxh3 ♖h2+ 41 ♘xh2 ♖xh2#.

MB27
Nunn – Smeets
Amsterdam 2006
32 ♖h4 caused instant resignation (in fact 32 ♖xg6+ also wins) as White is threatening 33 ♕h7+ ♔f8 34 ♕h8+! ♘xh8 35 ♖xh8#, and 32...♘xh4 is met by 33 ♘e7+! ♕xe7 34 ♕h7+ ♔f8 35 ♕h8#.

MB28
Potapov – Henrichs
Pardubice 2006
After the simple but not entirely obvious 27 ♘c5! Black resigned since 27...dxc5 allows 28 ♕xg6#, and otherwise the b7-bishop is lost.

MB29
Westerinen – Sigurjonsson
New York 1977
Obviously time is of the essence here and White was able to get his blow in first by sacrificing his queen: 25 ♕xg7+! ♔xg7 26 ♗d8+! ♔h8 (or 26...♔f7 27 ♗h5#) 27 ♖g8+! ♖xg8 28 ♗f6+ ♖g7 29 ♗xg7+ ♔g8 30 ♗xd4+ ♔f7 31 ♖f1+ ♔e7 32 ♗xb2 and Black resigned.

MB30
Bareev – Zsinka
Næstved 1988
13...♗f3! caused instant resignation. The threat is 14...♖h6 15 h3 ♗xg2, and if 14 gxf3, then 14...♖h6 15 ♖e1 ♕xh2+ 16 ♔f1 ♕h3+ 17 ♔g1 ♕h1#, while 14 ♖e1 is met by 14...♖g6 15 g3 ♕xh2+!.

Instead, after 13...♖h6 14 f3 ♕xh2+ 15 ♔f2 Black has won a pawn but the battle continues, while 13...♗xg2 14 ♔xg2 ♖h6 15 ♘g3 ♕h3+ 16 ♔f3 ♕g4+ 17 ♔g2 gives Black nothing better than perpetual check.

MB31
In this illustrative example Black is able to force a very pretty mate after

1...♖g8+ 2 ♔h6 ♕xh2+ 3 ♖h5 ♕d2+!
4 ♕xd2 ♖g6#.

MB32
Andreev – Dolukhanov
Leningrad 1935

a) After 1...♖xh2?! 2 ♖xh2 ♕xa3!
3 bxa3 (if 3 ♔b1?, then 3...♘c3+ 4
bxc3 ♔a8 wins) 3...♗xa3+ 4 ♔b1
♘c3+ 5 ♔a1 ♗b2+ 6 ♔xb2 ♘xd1+ 7
♔a2! (rather than 7 ♔c1? ♘xe3 8
fxg5) White can still fight.

b) The prosaic 1...♕c5! 2 ♕xc5
♗xc5 3 ♗xe4 ♗e3+ 4 ♔b1 ♖xd1+ 5
♖xd1 fxe4 6 ♗g1 ♗xg1 (not 6...♖h1?
7 fxg5) 7 ♖xg1 gxf4 is winning.

MB33
Petrosian – Pachman
Bled 1961

The great Tigran Petrosian revealed
his often hidden tactical depths with a
nice queen sacrifice. After 19 ♕xf6+!
♔xf6 20 ♗e5+ ♔g5 21 ♗g7! Pachman
resigned since the black king is trapped
and mate is unavoidable within a few
more moves.

MB34
Gargulak – Kogan
1909

After 1 ♖xe5! ♕xe5 2 ♘g6! the
main line continues 2...♕xd5? 3 ♘e7+
♔h8 4 ♕xh7+! ♔xh7 5 ♖h1+ and
mate follows. Obviously 2...♕xh2? 3
♘de7# is no improvement, but Black
could have tried to bail out by 2...hxg6
3 ♕xe5 (not 3 ♖h1? f6) 3...cxd5 with a
reasonable game.

MB35
Wells – Berry
British Ch, Torquay 2002

Indeed he could, by playing ...♖a8
at some moment to prepare stalemate.

After 43 ♖xg6 ♗xg6 44 ♖xg6 ♖h2
45 ♖xf6 ♖xe2 46 ♖f8 ♖a2+ (46...♖a8
works here since 47 ♘xa8+ is met by
47...♔d7 48 ♗xe2 ♕f2) 47 ♔b3 it still
wasn't too late for 47...♖a8 48 ♖xa8
(if 48 ♘xa8+, then 48...♔d7 49 ♔xa2
♕f2+ is sufficient) 48...♖b2+ 49 ♔a3
♖a2+ 50 ♔xa2 ♕f2+ 51 ♔b3 ♕b2+
52 ♔xb2 stalemate.

MB36
Dimakiling – Godena
Calvia 2006

The surprising 35...♘c4+! deflected
the white queen from its post so that
after 36 ♕xc4 ♖f2! *(D)* White had no
good check.

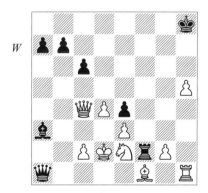

Black threatens 37...♗c1+ 38 ♔e1
♗xe3+ and 37...♕c1+ 38 ♔c3 ♕xe3+
and after 37 ♕a4 ♕c1+! 38 ♔c3 ♕xe3+
White resigned in view of 39 ♔c4 b5+.

MB37
Djukić – Cetković
Montenegro Team Ch,
Herceg Novi 2006

White supported his passed pawn by tactical means with 39 ♗xc4! ♔xc4 40 ♖c1+ ♔d5 41 ♖c8. Black now had nothing better than 41...♗xd7 and resigned after 42 ♖xb8 ♗a4 43 ♖g8 ♗c2 44 ♖xg5 ♔e6 45 ♖g7.

MB38
Krasenkow – Hebden
Port Erin 2006

41 ♖xg6+! caused instant resignation in view of 41...♔xg6 42 ♕c6+ ♕xc6 43 dxc6, when the c-pawn cannot be stopped.

MB39
Degraeve – Guidarelli
French Ch, Aix-les-Bains 2003

a) The fire of the queen, fianchettoed bishop and both rooks is aimed at g2.

b) Black continued 23...♗h4! 24 ♕xh4? (after 24 ♖d2 ♕xf3 25 ♕xf3 ♗xf3 26 g3 f5 27 ♖d7 {27 ♖f1 ♗c6} 27...f4 Black is better but it's still a fight) 24...♖xg2+ 25 ♖xg2 ♖xg2+ 26 ♔f1 ♕xf3+ and White resigned in view of 27 ♗f2 ♖g1+ 28 ♔xg1 ♕g2#.

MB40
Azmaiparashvili – Filippov
European Clubs Cup, Kallithea 2002

32 ♖xc6! bxc6 33 a5! was completely decisive since there was no way to protect a6. The game ended

33...♖b7 34 ♘c5 ♖e7 35 ♘xa6 ♔c8 36 ♘c5 ♔b8 37 a6 ♔a8 38 ♔e1 and Black resigned somewhat prematurely but certainly in a dead lost position since White can run Black out of moves on the kingside. For example, 38...f5 39 ♔d2 g5 40 e3 h6 41 h4 g4 42 h5, when Black must move a piece: 42...♖e8 (or: 42...♔b8 43 a7+ ♔a8 44 ♘a6; 42...♔h7 43 ♘e6 ♖h8 44 ♔c3, etc.) 43 ♘d7 ♖d8 44 ♘e5 ♖d6 45 ♔c3 and there's no defence.

MB41
Kasimdzhanov – Slobodjan
Bundesliga 2002/3

45 ♗xf6! gxf6 46 ♕g6! smashed through. 46...♕d6 was forced (since 46...♖d6 allows 47 ♖e8#, and 46...♘e7 is met by 47 ♕xf6+ ♔e8 48 ♕h8+ ♔d7 49 ♖d4+), and after 47 c5! ♕c7 48 ♕xf6+ ♔g8 49 ♕g6+ ♔f8 50 ♕xh6+ ♔g8 51 ♖e3 Black resigned.

MB42
Kovchan – Sadvakasov
Kharkov 2003

Yes, White can save the game. After 28 ♘d7+! ♗xd7 29 ♖xf7+ ♔e8 (29...♔xf7 30 ♕f6+ is also perpetual), 30 ♖f8+!! saved the day: 30...♖xf8 31 ♗h5+ ♖f7 32 ♗xf7+ ♔xf7 and they agreed a draw in view of the coming perpetual check.

MB43
Van Wely – Sutovsky
European Clubs Cup,
Rethymnon 2003

Indeed he can. After 26...♘xe4! 27 ♕xe4 ♖e8 then of course if 28 ♕xe8+, 28...♕xe8+ is check so White has no time for 29 ♖d8. Instead he tried to turn the tables with 28 ♖d8 immediately but 28...♕c4+! forced instant resignation.

MB44
Moldoianov – Samochanov
1974

1 ♖xa5? ♔g3 gives Black has excellent drawing chances, but White was able to set up a beautiful mating-net with 1 ♖g6! a4 2 ♔e3 a3 3 ♔f4 a2 4 ♖g3 ♗e6 5 ♖h3+! ♗xh3 6 g3#.

MB45
Wittmann – Am. Rodriguez
Prague 1980

White could have saved himself with a nice stalemate combination: 1 ♖xb3+! ♔xa2 2 ♖a3+! ♔b2 (not 2...♔b1?? 3 ♕d1+ while if 2...♔xa3, then 3 ♕d3+! forces stalemate immediately) 3 ♕b5+! ♔xa3 (3...♔c1? 4 ♖a1+ ♔d2 5 ♕xa5+) 4 ♕d3+! ♕xd3 stalemate.

MB46
Devereaux – Snape
British Ch, Swansea 2006

16 ♖d8+ ♘xd8 17 ♘d6+ blasted through. After 17...♔d7 18 ♘xb7 ♗xb7 19 ♖d1+ ♗d5 20 c4 g5 21 ♕e4 ♔c6 22 ♕d4 Black resigned.

MB47
Miles – Browne
Lucerne Olympiad 1982

White finished matters off with a classic double bishop sacrifice: 18 ♗xh7+ ♔xh7 19 ♕h5+ ♔g8 20 ♗xg7 ♔xg7 (if 20...f6 or 20...f5, then 21 ♕h8+ ♔f7 22 ♗xf8 wins in either case since of course if 22...♖xf8, 23 ♕h7+ skewers king and queen) 21 ♕g5+ ♔h8 22 ♕f6+ ♔g8 23 ♖c4 and Black resigned.

MB48
Yakovenko – E. Berg
European Clubs Cup, Fügen 2006

White very much wants to play 30 ♖xe5 if possible and indeed it does work beautifully. After 30...♖xe5 31 ♕xf4+ *(D)*, we have:

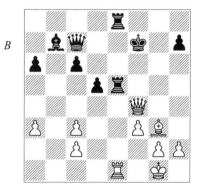

a) 31...♔g8 32 ♕g4+ ♕g7 (if 32...♔f7, then 33 ♗xe5 ♖xe5 34 ♕f4+ ♔e6 35 ♕h6+; or 32...♔h8 33 ♕d4) 33 ♕xg7+ ♔xg7 34 ♗xe5+ and White wins.

b) In the game Black tried 31...♔g6 but after 32 ♕g4+ ♖g5 (if 32...♔f6/f7, then 33 ♗xe5(+) ♖xe5 34 ♕f4+ as in line 'a') 33 ♖xe8 ♖xg4 (33...♕b6+ 34

♕d4 ♕xd4+ 35 cxd4 a5 would at least save the piece) 34 ♗xc7 ♖c4, 35 ♖b8 trapped the bishop. After 35...♖xc3 36 ♖xb7 ♖xc2 37 ♗e5 c5 38 g4 d4 39 ♖g7+ ♔h6 40 ♖g8 Black resigned.

Tougher Examples

TE01
Gofshtein – V. Mikhalevski
Israeli Ch, Tel-Aviv 2002
After 31 ♘h6+ ♔g7 32 ♕d4+! ♔xh6 33 ♕h4+ ♔g7 34 ♖e7+ ♖f7 35 ♖xd7 ♖xd7 White went on to win.

TE02
Korchnoi – Van der Stricht
European Team Ch, Plovdiv 2003
It certainly was. Not, of course 36...fxg6?? 37 ♕xh6#, but Black could continue the game with 36...♘xe5! 37 ♖xe6 ♘xd3! when, crucially, 38 ♖xh6+ gxh6+ is check. Since 38...♘f4+ is threatened, White loses a rook and Black emerges with a decisive material advantage.

TE03
Maksimenko – Miladinović
Bratto 2004
After 23...♘xe3! 24 fxe3 ♕xg3+ 25 ♔f1 (25 ♔e2 ♖xe3+ 26 ♔f1 ♖d1#) 25...♖d1+ 26 ♔e2 it looked as though White had escaped, but the very pretty 26...♖e1+! caused instant resignation.

TE04
Ruijgrok – Li Shilong
Hoogeveen 2004

The fianchettoed bishop aimed at the black king is menacing, and the white queen is well-centralized on d5, but White needs to involve more forces if he is to construct a serious attack. He did so with 22 ♘g5+! hxg5 (if 22...♔h8 23 ♘e6 fxg3 24 fxg3 ♕b6+ 25 ♔h1, the attack is overwhelming) 23 ♗e4+! g6 (or 23...♔h8 24 ♕xg5!) 24 ♗xg6+! and Black resigned in view of 24...♔xg6 25 ♕xg5+ ♔h7 26 ♕h5+ ♔g8 27 ♕h8+ ♔f7 28 ♕g7#.

TE05
In this example position with so many attacking pieces it's clearly time to strike and 1 ♘xf7! ♔xf7 2 ♗xf6! cuts through: 2...♕xc7 3 ♕h5+ ♔f8 (3...♔xf6 4 ♕g6#) 4 ♗xg7+ ♔xg7 5 ♕g6+ ♔f8 6 ♕xh6+ ♔f7 (6...♔g8 7 ♗h7+ ♔f7 {or 7...♔h8 8 ♗g6+ ♔g8 9 ♕h7+ ♔f8 10 ♕f7#} 8 ♕g6+ ♔f8 9 ♕g8#) 7 ♗g6+ ♔f6 8 ♗h7+ ♔f7 9 ♕g6+ ♔f8 10 ♕g8#.

TE06
Kasparian – Manvelian
Erevan 1939
White forced his opponent's king on a journey with 1 ♖xc6 ♗xc6 2 ♕c4+ ♔b7 3 ♕xc6+! ♔xc6 4 ♘e5++ ♔c5 5 ♘d3+ ♔d4 and then wrapped up with the quiet but deadly 6 ♔d2!.

TE07
Bannik – Cherepkov
USSR 1961
After 1...♖g5+ 2 ♖g2 ♕c5+ 3 ♕f2 ♖e2! White resigned in view of 4

♕xc5 ♖gxg2+ 5 ♔h1 ♖h2+ 6 ♔g1 ♖eg2#.

TE08
Nayer – Kornev
Tomsk 2006
The solution is only three moves long but it wasn't immediately obvious to me when I first saw it.

After 21 ♖xc6+! Black resigned at once, not waiting for 21...bxc6 22 ♕xc2! ♕xc2 23 ♖b8#.

TE09
Gozzoli – Phoobalan
World Junior Ch, Goa 2002
21 ♖e6! (not 21 ♘xf7?, which is refuted by both 21...♔xf7 and 21...♕xf3) 21...fxe6 22 ♗xe6+ ♔h8 (of course, if 22...♔f8, then 23 ♘xh7+) 23 ♘f7+ *(D)*.

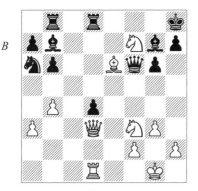

23...♔g8 (he could also consider 23...♕xf7 24 ♗xf7 ♖d7) 24 ♘xd8+ ♔f8 25 ♘xb7 ♖xb7 (or 25...♕xe6 26 ♕xa6 ♕d5 27 ♕xa7) 26 ♘xd4 and White was easily winning because

26...♕xd4 is met by 27 ♕f3+!. It ended 26...♘c7 27 ♗b3 ♖b8 28 ♘e6+ ♘xe6 29 ♕d6+ 1-0.

TE10
Gogolev – Varshavsky
1967
Given that this is a tactics book you should immediately have thought about stalemate here and indeed Black escaped with 1...♖d1+ 2 ♔h2 ♕g1+ 3 ♔g3 ♖d3+! 4 ♕xd3 ♕e3+! 5 ♕xe3 stalemate.

TE11
Golubev – Knoppert
Belgian League 2002/3
24 ♖xf7! (but not 24 ♖xd8? ♖xd8 25 ♗g5 bxc3 26 ♗f6 ♕d4+ and Black wins) 24...♔xf7 25 ♕h7+ ♔f6 (or 25...♔e8 26 ♖xd8+! ♔xd8 27 ♗g5+ ♔e8 28 ♕e7#) 26 ♖d2! (not 26 h4? ♗b6). This is actually the most difficult move since White must check carefully that after the quiet move there is no way out. There isn't and Black resigned in view of 26...♖f7 27 ♕h8+ ♖g7 (27...♔e7 28 ♕xd8#) 28 ♕f8+ ♖f7 29 ♖f2#.

TE12
Kariakin – Kosteniuk
Match (4), Brissago 2003
a) After 30 ♕xa6 ♖xc1+ 31 ♖xc1 ♖xa6 32 ♖c8+ ♕e8! 33 ♖xe8+ ♔f7 Kariakin finished matters with another beautiful move: 34 ♖a8!!.

b) Black can improve by 30...♖cb8 31 ♕d3 ♗xb3 32 ♖xb3 e4!? 33 fxe4 fxe4 34 ♕e3 ♕d5 with counterplay. And even after exchanging on c1, 31...♖f8 was a better chance.

Sadly it seems therefore that in the diagram the prosaic 30 ♖xc8+ ♖xc8 31 ♕xa6 was objectively stronger.

TE13
Vasquez – Jaime Montalvan
Malaga 2003

24 ♕xg7+! ♔xg7 25 ♖hg1+ and now:

a) In the game Black continued 25...♔f6 but perished after 26 ♗g5+ ♔e5 27 ♖de1+ ♔d4 28 ♗e3+ ♔e5 29 f4+ ♔f6 30 ♗d4+ ♔e7 31 ♖g7+, when he resigned due to the imminent mate.

b) 25...♗g3!? would have avoided the immediate mate but after 26 ♖xg3+ ♔f8 27 ♗h6+ ♔e7 28 ♗g5+ ♔d6 29 ♗xd8 ♖xd8 30 ♘xd5 the ending is easily winning.

TE14
Apicella – C. Bauer
French Ch, Aix-les-Bains 2003

Although the open h-file looks worrying, Black seems to be defending himself. However, White shattered this illusion with two mighty blows: 29 ♗xg5! ♗xg5 30 ♕f6+!! and Black resigned in view of 30...♗xf6 31 ♖g3+ and mate in two more moves.

TE15
Cu. Hansen – Lehtinen
Nordic Ch, Århus 2003

29 ♗a6 is the obvious move but after 29...bxa6, White must avoid 30

♕xa6+? ♔d7, when the king escapes. Instead 30 ♗a5! closed the net. Black tried 30...♖d8 but after 31 ♕xa6+ ♔d7 32 ♕b7+ ♔e8 33 ♗xd8 ♕g5 34 ♖e1 he resigned.

TE16
Korneev – Prasad
Port Erin 2003

44 ♖h8!! threatens 45 ♘f5+ (but not 44 ♖xa8 ♖xa8 45 ♘d5 ♕h4; while if 44 ♖b8, 44...♗b7 45 ♕c1 ♖a8 46 ♖c7 ♖c6! hangs on). Now:

a) If 44...♔xh8, then 45 ♘f5 gxf5 (or 45...♕f8 46 ♖c8! ♕xc8 47 ♕h6+ ♔g8 48 ♕g7#) 46 ♕h6+ ♔g8 47 ♖c8+.

b) So Black tried instead 44...♕g5 but resigned after 45 ♖cc8. There was no good defence against the threat of 46 ♘d5 ♕xd2 47 ♖cg8#. For example, 45...♕f4 46 ♖cg8+ ♔f6 47 ♖xa8 ♖xa8 48 ♘d5+, 45...♖xa3 46 ♖cg8+ ♔f6 47 ♕xd6# or 45...f6 46 ♘f5+ gxf5 47 ♖cg8+.

TE17
McShane – Nakamura
Pamplona 2003

White played 37 g3 and later drew. Instead the pretty 37 ♗h6! would have won immediately. The threat is 38 ♕h8# and after 37...♕xh6, 38 ♘e7+ ♔h7 39 ♕f7+ ♕g7 40 ♕f5+ ♔h8 41 ♕h5+ ♕h7 42 ♕e8+ finishes matters.

TE18
Tomba – Zhukova
Saint Vincent 2004

23...♗f5! caused immediate resignation in view of 24 ♗xf5 ♕e1+ or 24 ♕d2 ♕xf2+, etc.

TE19
Arbakov – Levin
Berlin 1994

After 24 ♖xg7! Black tried to bail out with 24...♕xe4 but only lasted half a dozen more moves: 25 ♖xf7 ♕g6 26 ♗e5+ ♘xe5 27 ♕xe5+ ♔g8 28 ♖f6 ♕g7 29 ♖d3 ♔h8 30 ♖g3 ♖d5 31 ♖f8+ 1-0. Instead 24...♗xg7 is critical but after 25 ♗h6+ ♔h8 26 ♕g5 f5 27 ♕f6+ ♔g8 28 ♖d3 f4 29 ♗xf4 ♖d7 (or 29...♕f7 30 ♖g3+ ♔f8 31 ♕h6+ ♔e8 32 ♖g7) 30 ♕xe6+ ♔h8 31 ♕xc4 White is easily winning.

TE20
Chiburdanidze – Polovnikova
Krasnoturinsk 2004

The first two moves of White's attack were fairly obvious: 23 ♘b6+ ♘xb6 24 axb6 a6 but it now required some flair to realize that after 25 ♖xa6+ bxa6 26 ♗xa6 Black is completely helpless. The game concluded 26...fxe4 27 ♖a1 e3+ 28 ♔e1 1-0.

TE21
Sandipan – Tiviakov
Ottawa 2007

After 22 ♗f6!! gxf6 (refusing the sacrifice doesn't help: 22...♘ac7 23 ♘xg7 ♘xg7 24 ♕h6 or 22...g6 23 ♕h6 ♘ac5 24 ♖bd1 ♕c7 25 ♖d4) 23 ♕h6! Black is helpless against the threats either to play ♕xf6 or to bring

up a rook. The game ended 23...♘ac5 (if 23...♗b7, then 24 ♕xf6 ♘ac5 25 ♘h6+ ♔f8 26 ♗xe6 ♘xe6 27 ♘f5 ♔g8 28 ♖xe6 fxe6 29 ♘h6#) 24 ♖bd1! ♕b7 (or 24...♕c7 25 ♖d4 ♘e4 26 ♖exe4 dxe4 27 ♖xe4 and mate follows) 25 ♖d4 ♘e4 26 ♖exe4! dxe4 27 ♕xf6 ♕c7 28 ♘h6+ ♔f8 29 ♕h8+ ♔e7 30 ♘f5# (1-0).

TE22
Rehurek – J. Johansson
Olomouc 2002

After 38...♖xg3! 39 ♗xh5 ♖h3!! there was no escape.

TE23
Rotlewi – Rubinstein
Lodz 1907/8

It's more than likely that the winner of TE22 had at some point seen this classic example.

Rubinstein won in just four sizzling moves, starting with 22...♖xc3!. Then:

a) 23 ♗xc3 allows 23...♗xe4+ 24 ♕xe4 ♕xh2#.

b) 23 ♗xb7 ♖xg3 and the black attack continues with a material advantage to boot – in fact 24 ♖f3 (or 24 ♗f3 ♘xh2, winning) 24...♖xf3 25 ♗xf3 ♘f2+ 26 ♔g1 (or 26 ♔g2 ♕h3+ 27 ♔g1 ♘e4+ 28 ♔h1 ♘g3#) 26...♘e4+ 27 ♔f1 ♘d2+ 28 ♔g2 ♘xf3 29 ♕xf3 ♖d2+ completes matters.

c) The game concluded 23 gxh4 ♖d2!! 24 ♕xd2 (if 24 ♗xb7, then 24...♖xe2 25 ♗g2 ♖h3 and other defences are no better) 24...♗xe4+ 25 ♕g2 ♖h3!! and White resigned.

TE24
Savchenko – Zavgorodny
Illichevsk 2006

White has multiple forces aimed at the enemy monarch but must still fix on a specific target. 19 ♕xh7+? ♔xh7 20 ♖h3+ ♔g6 21 ♖g3+ is only a draw and 19 ♖h3 h6 isn't immediately convincing.

But he hit home at once with 19 ♕g6!. Of course now 19...hxg6 allows 20 ♖h3# while 19...♘c6 is met by 20 ♖h3 h6 21 ♗f5 ♔g8 22 ♖xh6 ♘e5 23 ♖h8+ ♔xh8 24 ♕h7#. So Black tried 19...♗c8 but resigned at once after 20 ♖h3, not waiting for 20...h6 21 ♖xh6+.

TE25
Berkes – Zhang Pengxiang
Taiyuan 2006

After 28...♖h8! 29 ♗xa7+ (or 29 ♕xc4 ♖g7) 29...♔a8! 30 ♕xc4 ♖g7 there was absolutely no escape and the game ended 31 ♖d4 ♗f4# (0-1).

TE26
Visser – Speelman
London/Crowthorne 2006

24...♘xf2! coordinated the black forces. Now 25 ♖xf2 fxe4 and 25 ♖xe7 ♘xe4+ 26 ♔g2 ♖g7 are unpalatable, so my opponent tried 25 ♗f3 but there followed 25...♘e4+ 26 ♔h1 ♖xg3! 27 ♕xe7 ♕g1+ 28 ♖xg1 ♘f2# (0-1).

TE27
Mortensen – L. Karlsson
Esbjerg 1988

The stunning 20...♖xf3 21 ♖xf3 ♘b4!! caused instant resignation since after 22 axb4 ♗a4 there is absolutely no defence.

TE28
Baburin – King
British League (4NCL) 2003/4

24...♕xd4! wins a crucial pawn. In the game White refused the sacrifice but after 25 ♖e2 ♕f6 Black won a dozen moves later. He couldn't take the queen: 25 exd4 ♖xe1+ 26 ♔g2 ♘e3+ 27 ♔f3 ♗g4+ 28 ♔f4 ♖xf2+ 29 ♔g5 (or 29 ♔e5 ♘c4#) 29...♖f5+ 30 ♔h4 ♖h5#.

TE29
Cabrera – Shipov
Dos Hermanas
(Internet knockout) 2003

The very beautiful desperado 31 ♕g5!! cements White's advantage. If 31...♕b7, then 32 ♕xh5 with a second pawn for the exchange and a continuing attack. In the game Black tried 31...♖xg5 but after 32 ♖xc6 ♖g6 33 ♘xd4 ♘xd4 34 ♖c5 White went on to win.

TE30
Van Wely – Acs
Hoogeveen 2002

15...♖e6! included the rook in the attack, threatening 16...♖h6 followed by mate.

16 ♔g1 is met by 16...♕g5+. White could also try 16 ♗g6 but 16...♖xg6 17 ♘xg6 hxg6 18 ♘f4 g5 is decisive.

Instead Van Wely took the rook but after 16 ♘xe6 ♗f5+ 17 ♔g1 ♕h2+ 18 ♔f1, 18...♗g3! closed the net and White resigned.

TE31
King – Emms
London (Staunton Memorial) 2003

Of course White wants to play 31 ♖xf6. It was hard to calculate in time-trouble but after 31...♖xe2 32 ♖f7+ White wins:

a) 32...♔xg6 33 ♖1f6+ ♔g5 34 ♖f5+ ♔xg4 (34...♔g6 35 ♗h5#) 35 ♖g7+ ♔h3 36 ♖h5# is mate.

b) 32...♔g8 33 ♗e6 and Black has no defence; e.g., 33...♖e8 (33...♖b6 34 ♖f8++ ♔g7 35 ♖1f7+ ♔xg6 36 ♖g8+ ♔h5 37 ♗g4#) 34 ♖e7+ ♔h8 35 ♖h7#.

TE32
Lutikov – Gurgenidze
Sverdlovsk 1957

With four queens on the board and nether king very happy, attack is paramount.

Black found a way through to the enemy monarch with 45...♕xb2!! 46 ♖xb2 (if 46 ♕xf8+, then 46...♖xf8 47 ♖xb2 ♕xb2 is winning) 46...♖a3+ 47 ♔xb4 ♕xb2+ 48 ♔b3 ♖xb3+ 49 axb3 ♕f2 50 ♔a4 g3 and White resigned.

TE33
Najdorf – Kotov
Mar del Plata 1957

21 ♗c2!! takes aim at h7. 21...♖xc2 22 ♗xf6 and now 22...♗xf6 loses to 23

♕xh7+ ♔f8 24 ♕xc2. Instead 22...h6 is a tougher defence but 23 ♕h5 ♖f8 (23...♗xf6 24 ♕xf7+ ♔h7 25 ♖xh6+ ♔xh6 26 ♕g6#) 24 ♗xg7! (24 ♕xh6? doesn't work) crashes through; for example, 24...♗g5 25 ♗xh6 ♕f6 26 ♕xg5+ ♕xg5 27 ♗xg5 f6 28 ♗h6, etc.

TE34
Alekhine – Verlinsky
Odessa 1918

Although the solution is just a single move, I found it very hard to find when I revisited this position recently. The splendid 24 ♕d1! defends everything. After 24...♕a5 25 ♕xe2 ♕xe5 26 ♖d5 Black resigned.

TE35
Van Beek – Speelman
Gibraltar 2007

18 ♖xe6!! crashes into Black's kingside fortifications. 18...fxe6 (objectively 18...♗f8 is better but White is a whole pawn up) 19 ♘xg7! (not 19 ♘xh6+ gxh6 20 ♗xh6 ♘f8!) and now:

a) Here I tried 19...♗f8 and after 20 ♘xe8 ♖xe8 21 ♕g6+ ♗g7 22 ♗xh6 ♖e7 was very lucky to hold the game: 23 ♗f4 ♘f8 24 ♕g5 ♘8h7 25 ♕g6 ♘f8 26 ♕g5 ♘8h7 27 ♕g6? (27 ♕h4 ♕xc4 28 h6 ♗h8 29 ♕g3+ ♔f8 30 ♗d6 ♔e8 31 ♘e5 ♕xd4 32 ♗xe7 ♔xe7 33 ♘g6+ ♔d7 34 ♘xh8 is winning) 27...♘f8 ½-½.

b) The main line after 19...♔xg7 is 20 ♗xh6+ ♔h8 21 ♗g7+!! (21 ♘g5 ♘f8 22 ♘f7+ ♔g8 23 ♕g3+! also wins) 21...♔xg7 (or 21...♔g8 22 ♕g6, etc.) 22 ♕g6+ ♔h8 23 ♘g5 ♖f8 24 h6 and mate next move.

TE36
Eliskases – Henneberger
Bad Liebwerda 1934

26 ♗d5+ ♕f7! (not 26...♔f8? 27 ♖f4+ ♖xf4 28 exf4 and wins; 26...♔g7 is playable but after 27 ♕xe5+ ♕xe5 28 ♗xe5+ ♔h6 29 ♖h4+ ♔g5 30 ♗f4+ ♔f6 31 ♖h3 g5 32 ♖h6+ ♔g7 33 ♖e6 gxf4 34 gxf4 White has the advantage in the ending) and now:

a) Here White played 27 ♗xf7+?? and after 27...♔f8! he resigned.

b) Instead 27 ♖xg6+! was the only move, making room for the king to run. 27...♔f8! (if 27...hxg6, 28 ♗xf7+ followed by g4 now wins: 28...♔xf7 29 g4) 28 g4 ♕xg6 (not 28...♕f2 29 ♖g8+) 29 ♕xe5. This is the position I wanted you to reach. After 29...♕xg4 30 ♕b8+ ♔e7 31 ♕c7+ ♕d7 32 ♕e5+ ♔d8 33 ♕b8+ Black should accede to the perpetual.

TE37
Botvinnik – Smyslov
World Ch (18), Moscow 1958

Botvinnik played 23 ♗h3 and after 23...♘e5 later drew.

Instead the beautiful 23 ♘d4!! disrupts Black's defences. 23...♘xd4 (if 23...cxd4, then 24 ♗d5+ ♖xd5 25 ♖e8 wins immediately) 24 ♖e7 ♘e2+ (it is best to play this immediately; after 24...♖f7 25 ♗d5 ♘e2+ 26 ♖7xe2 it is over) 25 ♖1xe2 ♖f7 and now White is winning after either the simple 26

♖xc2 ♖d1+ 27 ♗f1 ♖xe7 28 ♖d2 or 26 ♗f1 ♕xc3 27 ♖xf7 ♔xf7 28 ♕xh7+ ♔f8 29 ♖e7.

TE38
Topalov – Lutz
Dortmund 2002

27 ♘f6+! gxf6 28 ♖d8+ ♖xd8 29 ♖xd8+ ♔h7 30 ♕f8. In a game it would be easy to reach here and you would be fairly confident that White was winning but want to calculate further to make sure.

a) Lutz tried 30...♔g6 and after 31 ♕g8+ ♔h5 32 ♕g7! f5 (if 32...♕b4, then 33 ♖d5+! ♗xd5 34 g4+ ♔h4 35 ♕xh6#) 33 ♖d4 ♗c8 (33...♗xb3 34 g4+ ♔h4 35 gxf5+) 34 g3! Black resigned.

b) 30...h5 was also a plausible defence but after 31 ♕h8+ ♔g6 32 ♖g8+ ♔f5 33 ♕xh5+ ♔f4 34 ♖d8! White cuts off the black king's escape. There are various defensive tries, of which I would be most concerned about 34...♗xb3 when in fact White can mate with checks but the most practical is 35 ♕h6+ ♔e5 36 ♕e3+ ♔f5 37 ♕d3+ ♔e5 38 cxb3, when it's obviously all over.

TE39
Short – Stefanova
British League (4NCL) 2002/3

14 ♖xf7! is fairly obvious but the consequences are certainly not. After 14...♖xf7 15 ♘xf7 ♘xc3 16 ♘xd8 ♘xd1 17 ♖xd1 White has won a pawn, but the knight is trapped at present.

However, the king can't approach since 17...♔f8 is met by 18 ♖f1+ and 19 ♘f7. Moreover, 17...♗xh3 allows 18 ♘xb7, while the rook ending after 17...♗g4 18 hxg4 ♖xd8 looks foul.

Black tried 17...a5 but after 18 ♖f1 a4 19 bxa4 ♖xa4 20 ♖f7! ♖c4 21 c3 b5 22 ♖e7 ♔f8 23 ♖xe4 Short was in full control and went on to win.

TE40
Kasparov – Kramnik
Novgorod 1994

Kasparov found the splendid 27 h5!!. Then the following lines all lose: 27...♖g7 28 ♕h6; 27...♕a5 28 hxg6 ♕a1+ 29 ♔c2 ♘b4+ 30 cxb4 ♖c8+ 31 ♘c5; 27...♖xg4 28 ♕xg4 ♖g8 29 ♕xg8+ ♔xg8 30 ♖xb6 ♘xb6 31 ♖g3+ ♔h8 32 ♘c5; 27...fxe6 28 hxg6 ♘xf4 29 ♖xh7+ ♔g8 30 ♖xb6; 27...♖xe6 28 hxg6 ♘xf4 29 ♖xh7+ ♔g8 30 gxf7+ ♔f8 31 ♖h8+ ♔xf7 32 ♗xe6+ ♘xe6 33 ♖xb6; or 27...♖gg8 28 ♖xd5! ♖xe6 29 ♗xe6 ♕xe6 30 ♖d6.

The main line is 27...♘xf4, and continues 28 hxg6 ♕xd6 (if 28...♘d3+, then 29 ♖hxd3! exd3 30 gxf7 wins) 29 ♖xh7+ ♔g8 30 gxf7+ ♔xh7 31 fxe8♕ ♘xe6 32 ♗f5+! ♔g7 33 ♕g6+ ♔f8 34 ♕xf6+ ♔e8 35 ♗xe6. A world-class player like Kasparov could well get to here from the diagram and would

surely stop since White is a pawn up and there are no checks. Kramnik now blundered with 35...♕f8? and re-signed without waiting for 36 ♗d7+. 35...e3 is a better try but also loses.

TE41
Asauskas – Malishauskas
Lithuanian Ch, Vilnius 2004

The beautiful 19 ♕f6+!! smashed through and after 19...♗xf6 20 gxf6+ ♔g8 (or 20...♕xf6 21 exf6+ ♔xf6 22 ♗xc5, winning easily) 21 ♖xh7! ♔xh7 22 ♖h3+ ♔g8 23 ♗h6! ♕c7 24 f4! Black resigned.

TE42
Geller – Karpov (variation)
USSR Ch, Moscow 1976

This position occurs after Garry Kasparov's suggested improvement (in *My Great Predecessors*) on Karpov's play during the game. However, the Russian player Sergei Sorokhtin, working with computer assistance, uncovered this staggering variation: 26 ♘g6+!! ♖xg6 27 ♘h7+ ♔e7 28 ♖b1! ♖a7 (otherwise ♖b7+ decides) 29 ♕d6+! ♕xd6 30 exd6+ ♔d7 31 ♖b8! (threatening 32 ♘f8+ ♔c6 33 ♖b6#) 31...♔c6 32 ♘f8 ♖b7 (or 32...♖a6 33 d7) 33 ♖c8+ ♔b5 34 c6 and the pawns are unstoppable.